D0863000

Rainbow Lorikeets

This publication is Copyright 2013 by EKL Publishing. All products, publications, software and services mentioned and recommended in this publication are protected by trademarks. In such instance, all trademarks & copyright belong to the respective owners.

The moral rights of the author has been asserted

British Library Cataloguing in Publication Data

A catalogue record for this book is available from the British Library

ISBN 978-1-909820-22-7

Disclaimer and Legal Notice

Rainbow Lorikeets

The Complete Owner's Guide on How to Care For Rainbow Lorikeets

Facts on habitat, breeding, lifespan, behavior, diet, cages, talking and suitability as pets

Foreword

Hello and thank you for buying my book.

In this book you will find some wonderful information to help you care for your Rainbow Lorikeet. I've included in this book information about Rainbow Lorikeet care, habitat cages, enclosure, diet, facts, set up, food, names, pictures, life span, breeding, feeding, cost and a care sheet. After reading this book you will be a lot more confident in looking after your Rainbow Lorikeet!

I have written this book using American spelling as that is what I'm used to. I have given measurements in both feet and inches/pounds and ounces and also in metric. I have also given costs in US$ and GBP. Both the measurements and costs are approximate guides. I have done my best to ensure the accuracy of the information in this book as at the time of printing.

I trust that after reading this book you will enjoy the experience of owning and looking after a Rainbow Lorikeet and that you have a wonderful time enjoying the pleasure they bring in the years to come!

All good wishes,

Rose Sullivan

Acknowledgements

I dedicate this book to my wonderful husband Marc for all his love and support over the last several months. His patience and encouragement means so much to me.

My children Mike and Cathy have been wonderful and their understanding and love for my passion has been so appreciated.

Table of Contents

Chapter 1: Introduction 1

    Commonly Used Terms 5

Chapter 2: Origin and Characteristics 8

    Vast Variety in the Lorikeet Family 9

    Physical Characteristics 9

        Tongues Equipped with Papillae.............................. 10

        Beaks.. 11

        Feet and Legs 11

        Temperament and Behavior 12

        High-Maintenance "Poop" 13

    Rainbow Lorikeets in the Wild 13

    Physical Description of Rainbow Lorikeets..................... 14

        Male or Female?... 15

        Size and Weight 16

        Personality as Pets... 16

        Hand-Raised Chicks.. 18

Chapter 3: Rainbow Lorikeets as Pets 19

    What to Know Before Buying 20

        Human Health Considerations 20

        Lorikeets Live a Long Time...................................... 20

        Lorikeets Need a Specialized Diet 21

        Vocal and Territorial Birds 22

        Hormonal Aggression 23

Lories Aren't Pet Store Birds 23

Aviaries and Breeders in the United States 24

Aviaries and Breeders in the United Kingdom 31

Lorikeet Buying Tips 32

Rainbow Lorikeets and Children 33

Rainbow Lorikeets and Other Pets 34

What About Wing Clipping? 36

Introducing a Second Lorikeet to the Household 39

Rainbow Lorikeets and Other Bird Species 40

Time Away from Your Lorikeet 40

Coming Home Again 42

Pros and Cons of Owning a Rainbow Lorikeet 43

Chapter 4: Daily Care 45

Shopping 46

Cage 46

Cage Skirts and Newspapers 48

If Possible Create an Outdoor Space 49

Ladders and Swings 50

A Good Variety of Perches 50

Intellectual Stimulation 51

Nectar Mix, Treats and Vitamins 51

Cuttlebone 53

Mineral Block 54

Lava Stone 54

Food and Water Dishes 55

Bath 56

Travel Carrier 57

Arranging Your Rainbow Lorikeet's Home 57

Picking the Right Cage Location 58

Cleaning Your Lorikeet's Cage 59

Handling Your Rainbow Lorikeet.......................... 60

Can Rainbow Lorikeets Talk?................................ 62

"Potty" Training a Lorikeet.................................... 63

Free Flying Time... 65

Nap Time and Sleeping... 66

Watch for Any Sign of Feather Plucking............... 66

Chapter 5: Quick Facts... 69

Excitement 70

Aggression 70

Nervousness 71

Relaxation 71

Sleeping.. 72

Preening and Bathing 72

Attention Displays.. 73

Vocalizations.. 74

Chapter 6: Health 75

Is My Rainbow Lorikeet Healthy?......................... 76

Is My Rainbow Lorikeet Unhealthy?..................... 78

Common Health Problems 80

Iron Storage Disease 80

Aspergillosis.. 82

Pacheco's Disease 83

Chlamydiosis.. 84

Scaly Face and Leg Disease.. 86

Feather Plucking 86

Bacterial and Yeast Contamination............................... 88

Candidiasis 88

Can Humans Be Allergic to Birds?................................ 90

Dander Pneumoconiosis.. 91

Bird Flu (Avian Influenza).. 92

Working with a Qualified Avian Veterinarian................. 93

Taking Your Bird to Meet the Vet 95

Pet Insurance 96

Chapter 7: Care Sheet 99

Overview.. 100

Housing 100

Cage Placement.. 101

Cage Cleaning 101

Transportation 102

Cage Accessories 102

Food 102

Cuttlebone, Mineral Block, Lava Stone 103

Vitamins... 103

Socialization... 103

Water.. 104

Signs of Illness 105

Chapter 8 – Breeding 106

Reasons to Hand Rear Lorikeet Chicks 107

Caring for Rainbow Lorikeet Chicks 108

What is a Brooder? 110

Hand Feeding Chicks 110

    Hand Feeding Formula 112

Weaning the Chicks 112

Leg Banding in Professional Aviaries 114

A Final Word on Breeding Rainbow Lorikeets 114

Chapter 9: Life After You 117

Finding a Permanent Home for Your Rainbow Lorikeet 120

Making it Legal 121

Chapter 10: Closing Thoughts 123

Chapter 11: Frequently Asked Questions 126

Chapter 12: Relevant Websites 131

    Shopping 131

Appendix 1 - CITES and Parrots 134

    Selected Works Cited 138

Glossary 140

Index 145

Photo Credits 152

Chapter 1: Introduction

There is no better description of a Rainbow Lorikeet than his own name. These medium-sized parrots are vibrantly colored, naturally arrayed in greens, reds, blues, yellows and blacks. When seen in a flock, they are nothing short of spectacular.

Their uniqueness hardly stops there. Unlike many other parrot species, Rainbow Lorikeets are "brush-tongued," existing primarily on a diet of nectar and fruit. This ability to efficiently draw liquid into their mouths also allows them to extract their primary water supply from dew and rainfall on the leaves of the trees in which they live.

Thanks to the enthusiasm of aviculturists, there are many color mutations of Lorikeets available. This in addition to the interchangeable use of the terms "Lory" and "Lorikeet", can make this a confusing companion species at first glance. Look again!

The reason there is such a wide variety speaks to the affable popularity of Lorikeets as companions. Comical by nature, social, agreeable and delightfully curious, these creatures make absolutely delightful pets.

There is, however, one serious caveat that must be discussed from the very beginning of your consideration of life with a Rainbow Lorikeet. By nature, these birds are designed to eat a liquid diet. The consequence is extremely liquid feces, which they tend to excrete at a 45-degree angle.

Cleaning up after a Lorikeet is a never-ending job, but one most people think is worth it for the experience of living with a highly intelligent and loving bird. There are some companies marketing various food products that are in theory designed to "improve" a Lorikeet's feces. That's just advertising speak for "constipate."

Lorikeets are what they are, and they must be accepted that way from the beginning. They are not a low-maintenance bird, and they aren't great talkers. If you want a parrot you can teach to talk, consider an African Grey.

That is not to say a Lorikeet can't or won't acquire language, but it is not a trait for which this species is singled out, and should not be your primary reason for bringing a Lorikeet home.

With any companion animal, regardless of species, it's extremely important to go into the relationship with correct expectations. In adopting a pet of any kind, you are assuming complete responsibility for the welfare of a living creature.

The purpose of this book is to provide an overview of living with and caring for a Rainbow Lorikeet. It is entirely possible for your bird to live as long as 30 years. Before you commit to that responsibility, for your sake, and for the bird's, you need to learn as much as you can about the species.

If, however, you decide you are equal to the challenge, the

trade-off will be the companionship and affection of one of nature's most beautiful and remarkable creatures.

Unlike dogs, that offer us a friendly wag of the tail, or cats who will purr or climb in our laps, birds have very different ways of expressing affection and communicating their wants and needs.

Rainbow Lorikeets are a loving, active and bright species and when you learn their language, they have a great deal to say and to share with their humans, whether they ever use our words or not!

Commonly Used Terms

aviary - An outdoor enclosed structure where companion birds are housed for their protection, or a facility where birds are bred for pleasure and for sale.

aviculture - The keeping of birds as companion animals and all the tasks associated with their husbandry.

beak – A bird's upper and lower jaw together form the beak, which is bright orange in Rainbow Lorikeets and elongated as an adaption for tearing chunks from ripe fruit rather than breaking seeds or nuts.

cage - The secure habitat in which companion birds are kept. Due to their size and activity level, Rainbow Lorikeets need "flight" or "conure" cages and should be allowed as much free flight time as possible, or have a secondary aviary habitat outdoors.

companion bird - Any species of bird that is kept as a pet and lives well in companionship with humans on a daily basis, including Rainbow Lorikeets.

crop - This sac-like structure is responsible for the preliminary stage of a bird's digestion. It sits below the esophagus and above the stomach. In chicks, the crop is clearly visible as a bulge on the bird's upper breast and is used as an indicator of the amount of food to give hand-raised babies.

cuttlebone - These chew toys have a consistency similar to pumice. They are a rich source of calcium, and help companion birds to keep their beaks worn down.

feather - Feathers comprise a bird's plumage. They are flat in structure, but vary in length according to location on the body. The longest feathers on a bird are typically found in the tail and in the ten long flight feathers present on each wing.

free flying - When a companion bird is allowed outside of the cage to fly without restraint around any secure area, the practice is referred to as free flying. Rainbow Lorikeets require a great deal of free flight time.

hormonal aggression - A trait seen in Rainbow Lorikeets that is the avian equivalent of the "terrible twos." It is at this point that the bird is maturing, and the effects of sexual hormones on its personality create a period of temporary aggression.

hand-rearing - Birds that are hand reared are removed from their parents' care early in life and fed by their human caregivers. This is a very important process of socialization in aviaries. Rainbow Lorikeets that have been hand reared are extremely well adjusted and make excellent pets.

Lorikeet (Lory) - These two terms are used interchangeably for a widely varied collection of brightly colored, medium-sized parrots indigenous to the islands of the South Pacific, Asia and Australia. The Rainbow Lorikeet is one of the most popular of these birds kept as a companion animal.

veterinarian - Medical professions who are trained in the care of animals are called veterinarians, however, not all veterinarians have been trained to care for birds. It is in your best interest and that of your Rainbow Lorikeet to find an "avian veterinarian" to provide the necessary healthcare procedures and interventions. A veterinarian is often referred to as a vet.

zoonotic – Disease that can be passed from any animal to human beings are said to "zoonotic" in nature. (Please see Chapter 6 - Health for a discussion of this topic as it relates to the Lorikeet species.)

Chapter 2: Origin and Characteristics

Narrowing down the world of Lories and Lorikeets is more difficult than you might imagine. The broad strokes are this. Both are parrots. Both come from the islands of the South Pacific and Australia.

In the most simplistic terms, Lorikeets are smaller and have longer tails; lories are larger and have shorter tails. Both belong to the family psittacidae and the sub-family loriinae.

Vast Variety in the Lorikeet Family

There are at least 50 species of Lories and Lorikeets and hundreds of sub-species. All are brush-tongued parrots that feed on nectar, pollen and fruit. Consequently, Lorikeets kept in captivity often suffer from poor nutrition and constipation. These birds cannot thrive on the seeds and pellets fed to "normal" parrots.

The difficulty sorting out Lorikeet species and sub-species is twofold. First, the terms Lory and Lorikeet tend to be used interchangeably. Second, aviculturists avidly breed the birds for color variations, which all sport unique, descriptive and confusing names.

For the purposes of this book, we will be talking about the "basic" Rainbow Lorikeet. Although specific Lorikeet sub-species may be listed, we are, on a whole, discussing one member of a family of vibrantly colored parrots found in a fantastic array of greens, blues, reds, yellows and blacks.

Physical Characteristics

All Lorikeets have a common set of distinctive physical characteristics and similarities of temperament and behavior. This does not mean, however, that all Lorikeets make good pets.

There are some sub-species that are threatened in the wild and protected by game laws, while others are simply too aggressive and loud to be kept by aviculture hobbyists.

Tongues Equipped with Papillae

All Lorikeet sub-species have tongues that have evolved to support a diet of nectar, pollen and flowers. Both the length of the tongue itself and the hair-like structures or papillae that make it unique, vary according to the flowers on which the given species feeds.

The papillae at the tip of the tongue serve to gather nectar and pollen, which is drawn into the mouth and scraped off by a specialized fold of skin and swallowed. The longer the papillae on the tongue, the more efficiently the bird can collect nectar and pollen and the more integral blossoms are to the creature's diet.

Papillae are also used to drink water. Lorikeets can gather dew and raindrops from the leaves in high trees where they live. A typical parrot uses its lower jaw to scoop up water from the ground, but a Lorikeet can use all sources of moisture available to them, no matter how slight.

Beaks

The structure of a Lorikeet's beak, though similar to that of other parrots, is not adapted to cracking seeds and nuts. The upper jaw is longer and narrower. The beak is used primarily to bite out chunks of fresh fruit. With their tongues, the birds then squeeze the juice from the pulp and spit out the rest.

Feet and Legs

Some Lorikeet owners are a little startled at first by just how much time their birds spend upside down. This is actually completely normal. Lorikeets have powerful legs and feet. Their nails are perfect for clinging securely in the most unlikely places. It may be a strange perspective on the world, but it's uniquely Lorikeet and since these are happy, gregarious birds, maybe they know something we don't!

Temperament and Behavior

Lorikeets are packed full of personality, and when they're in a flock, they put on a high-energy, boisterous show. Their fearless outlook on life can make Lorikeets a little difficult as roommates when kept with birds of other species. It's not out of the realm of possibility for a Lorikeet to be a bit of a bully.

While we might think the bird / cat "thing" is a matter of instinct, Lorikeets didn't get the message. Many a horrified owner has watched as their tough-chirping little bird gets right up in a cat's face and almost dared the feline to do something about it. Lorikeets don't always display good sense relative to their diminutive size!

However, feathered daredevils or not, Lorikeets are terrifically entertaining, and for first-time parrot owners, quite a handful. This is not a little guy who is going to sit in his cage and just watch what's going on. A Lorikeet is an executive at heart. He wants to be part of running the show. If you don't want an interactive bird, with an opinion about what you're doing, don't get a Lorikeet!

High-Maintenance "Poop"

Because Lorikeets primarily eat nectar, their feces are much more liquid than that of other birds. Also, they defecate at a 45-degree angle, doing what some aviculturists describe as "painting the wall."

Make no mistake, Lorikeets are work, and since they need a lot of time outside of the cage that means a much larger area for you to keep clean. It is possible to housebreak a Lorikeet to a degree, but high-maintenance poop is part of the deal. Know this going in.

Rainbow Lorikeets in the Wild

In the wild, both Lories and Lorikeets are part of large flocks that fly between islands of the South Pacific,

Southeast Asia and Australia in search of food. In Australia, they are regarded as a pest capable of decimating 70 to 90% of a fruit crop.

Wild Rainbow Lorikeets follow blooming eucalyptus flowers along the coast. Setting a pet Rainbow Lorikeet free in Australia is illegal. In addition to decimating crops, mated pairs of Lorikeets will aggressively drive other birds off their feeding grounds.

The International Union for Conservation of Nature (IUCN) lists almost all Lories and Lorikeets as "least concern" although there are three endangered species: the Red and Blue Lory, the Rimitara Lorikeet and the Ultramarine Lorikeet.

Physical Description of Rainbow Lorikeets

The Rainbow Lorikeet's name is well chosen. These medium-sized parrots are a study in brilliant colors starting with the brilliant blue head sitting above a yellowish green collar.

The wings, back and tail are all deep green. The red chest will have blue-black barring, with deep green on the belly. The thighs and rump are yellow with green barring. The underside of the wing, visible only in flight, is red with a prominent yellow bar.

Juvenile Rainbow Lorikeets have a black beak that brightens to an eye-catching orange in adults.

Male or Female?

Visually there is almost no difference in the appearance of cocks and hens. People who are familiar with Rainbow Lorikeets can distinguish the genders by behavior and extremely minute differences in coloration, but this takes a very practiced eye.

The principal differences are that males have more dark orange on the breast, whereas in females the breast bleeds from yellow to orange. Additionally, males have squarer features, while the hens have more rounded heads.

Some breeders determine the gender of their birds through DNA testing before offering them for sale. For purposes of keeping these birds as pets, gender makes no difference.

Unless you plan on breeding Lorikeets, the species is best housed alone and both genders are equally playful and agreeable.

Size and Weight

Rainbow Lorikeets will range in length from 10 to 15 inches (25.4 to 38.1 centimeters) and have a wingspan of roughly 6.7 inches (17 centimeters). Their weight will vary in a range of 2.6 to 5.5 ounces (73.7 to 156 grams.)

Personality as Pets

When kept as pets, Rainbow Lorikeets have a tendency to bond most deeply with one person, regarding their human as their "mate." This can result in jealous and possessive behavior if the bird doesn't feel it's getting enough of your attention.

When Lorikeets are kept as a family pet, it's important for every person in the household to cultivate a relationship with the bird.

This strategy cuts down on any aggression, and makes it possible for everyone to participate in caring for the bird's daily needs.

It's not hard to fall in love with a Rainbow Lorikeet. By nature, they're feathered clowns who prefer having a ringside seat for whatever is going on around them.

A Lorikeet almost always has an opinion, and he's quite capable of making his voice heard.

This need for interaction is balanced by genuine sweetness and conviviality. Lorikeets are receptive to training, often intentionally comical and openly affectionate.

They are active, agile and delightfully whimsical, a fact enhanced by their habit of spending a great deal of time upside down. These birds stay busy all day, and will need lots of sturdy chew toys.

Hand-Raised Chicks

To have the best experience with a Rainbow Lorikeet as a pet from the day you bring your bird home, try to find one that has been hand-raised.

These birds are very well socialized to humans, and they have typically also been exposed to all manner of toys, activities, noises, situations in their environment and possibly even other animals.

Hand-raised birds are well adjusted, and less likely to suffer undue stress coming into a new home.

Chapter 3: Rainbow Lorikeets as Pets

Buying a Lorikeet on an impulse is a bad idea – for you and for the bird. Bringing any companion animal into your home means assuming long-term responsibility for the welfare of another living creature. You need to know as much as you possibly can about Lorikeets before you even think about buying one.

What to Know Before Buying

With a bird like a Rainbow Lorikeet, there are many things that must be weighed in advance of an adoption including: the longevity of the creature, its need for a specialized diet, the amount of noise it will make, and issues with territoriality and aggression.

Human Health Considerations

In this book we cover some of the common health issues experienced by Lorikeets and some of the zoonotic diseases i.e. a disease that can be transmitted from an animal to a human being. We have also touched on the issue of allergies that can be caused by companion birds such as people being allergic to the dander. Before making the decision to bring a companion bird into your life, we strongly recommend that you take advice from your doctor and veterinarian so that you have a full understanding of any risks to your own health.

Lorikeets Live a Long Time

While not as long-lived as some parrots, a well-cared for Lorikeet can easily reach 30 years of age.

The very first question you have to ask yourself is whether or not you are willing to potentially devote three decades of your own life to properly care for this bird no matter what changes in your life and in your family.

It is not at all uncommon for parrot owners to make provisions for their birds in their wills should they predecease their pet. If you are in your early 50s, your Lorikeet could still be with you when you reach 80.

Every decision you make about your lifestyle and living circumstances from the moment you bring the Lorikeet home, must include a consideration of the bird's welfare as well as your own.

Lorikeets Need a Specialized Diet

Rainbow Lorikeets need diets composed primarily of fruit and nectar. They do not eat seeds or pellets except as occasional treats which can often be offered as rewards during training.

In order to get the low-protein, low-iron nutrition they require, your Lorikeet will need fresh fruits, vegetables, sprout seeds and nectar prepared from commercial liquid or powder mixes.

The nature of this diet means that a healthy Lorikeet's stool is liquid. They make such a mess most owners use some kind of skirt on the cage to catch the excrement.

Clean-up is constant. Do NOT feed your Lorikeet a diet that

purports to "firm" its stool. Such preparations are intentionally designed to constipate the animal, which is not only unhealthy, but also leads to aggressive behavior.

Vocal and Territorial Birds

Rainbow Lorikeets are territorial and can be possessive about "their" special human. These birds do not bite as much as other species of Lories, but they are quite vocal, and when they're not happy about something, they will let out loud screeches and screams.

Hormonal Aggression

Depending on the age of your Lorikeet at adoption, you may have to endure the avian version of the Terrible Twos. Just like a human adolescent, Rainbow Lorikeets in this stage of life are filled with raging hormones. The birds get very "nippy" during this phase, so watch your fingers! This same kind of hormonal aggression often resurfaces when a bird is ready to mate and during molting.

Lories Aren't Pet Store Birds

It's very rare for a Lorikeet to show up in a pet store. Since it's actually a much better practice to buy a bird from an aviary, this fact is to your advantage. The breeder is not just the person from whom you will buy your Rainbow Lorikeet, but also the person on whom you should be able to call on for future advice.

Visit the aviary to see the birds and learn about them before you decide to buy. Ask a lot of questions, and expect to answer just as many, as they will want to see if you will make an appropriate owner for their pride and joy.

Most aviculturists love their birds, and they want to see them go to good homes. These people will be very happy to help you learn, but they may also be quick to tell you if you just don't seem like a good candidate to join their ranks as a bird owner.

Don't get offended. Listen to what they have to say. Breeders are people who make their homes in the company of multiple birds.

No one is going to know the reality of living with a Lorikeet more fully than your breeder, and no one will be a better friend and mentor to you if you do decide to take the plunge and welcome a Lorikeet into your own life.

Aviaries and Breeders in the United States

Alabama
Tweety Bird Aviary
Huntsville, AL
http://www.tweetybirdaviary.com

Irena's Aviary
Blountsville, AL
www.eparrots.com

Arkansas
Fancy Feathers Aviary and Supplies
Little Rock, AR
501-453-4574

California
EMR Exotic Bird Breeder
San Diego, CA
www.emrexoticbirdbreeder.com

Melzano's Parrot Place
San Diego, CA
www.melzanosparrotplace.com

Feathered Nest
Northern CA, CA 95688
925-698-0191

Ara Aviaries California
28115 dorothy dr.
Agoura Hills Los Angeles, CA 91301
805-338-3549

Cedar Hill Birds
Lodi, CA 95240
http://www.cedarhillbirds.com

Ozark Exotics
Huntington Beach , CA
714-248-6827

Connecticut
Diane's Parrot Place
RT. 6 and RT. 61
Woodbury, CT 06798
http://dianesparrotplace.weebly.com

Florida
Best Bird Aviary
Summerfield, FL
www.thebestbird.com

Lone Palm Aviary
West Palm Beach, FL
www.lpbirds.com

Birds 4 You
Trinity, FL
www.birds4you.org

Featherheads
Lithia, FL 33547
(813) 679-4961

Feather's Bird Shoppe, Inc.
Reddick, FL 32686
352-369-0677

Georgia
Thunderbirds USA
Atlanta, GA
www.thunderbirdsusa1.com

East Coast Birds
Saint Marys, GA 31558
912-674-4841

Iowa
Zimmerman Pets
Sioux City, IA 51108
http://www.zimmermanpets.com

Louisiana
Cajunbait2000
Opelousas, LA 70570
337-255-3168

Missouri
Gateway Aviaries
St. Louis, MO 63119
314-374-1876

North Carolina
Lone Eagle Aviaries
Leasburg, NC 27291
703 606-1884

Nebraska
Love-A-Lop- Farm
Allen, NE 68710
www.lovealop.com

New Hampshire
CoooCooo's Nest
Derry, NH
www.cooocoooosnest.com

Parrot Safari
Londonderry, NH 03053
www.parrotsafari.com

New Jersey
World of Birds
Chester, NJ
www.worldofbirds.net

Birds by Joe LLC
Middlesex, NJ
www.birdsbyjoe.com

New York
Maria's Birds
North Tonawanda, NY
www.mariasbirds.com

For Birds Only
Mineola, NY 11501
www.forbirdsonlyny.com

Ohio
In a Pickle Parrots
Broadview Heights, OH
www.inapickleparrots.com

BirdWalk
549 Liberty St
Painesville, OH 44077
www.birdwalkstore.com

Oklahoma
Sooner Parrot Place
Oklahoma City, OK 73135
www.soonerparrotplace.com

Oregon
The Parrot Patch
Eugene, OR 97404
541-463-9564

Pennsylvania
Birds by Stephanie
Aliquippa, PA 15001
(724) 417-8146

Jr's Feathered Friends
Kunkletown, PA 18058
610-895-4092

Tennessee
The Bird Hut, Dickson, TN
www.the-bird-hut.com

Adventure Birds of Bom Aqua
9600 Highway 46
Bon Aqua, TN 37025
931-670-3204

Texas
Bayoubirdnest.Com
Beaumont, TX 77713
409-347-8221

Jadies Birdnest
Katy, TX 77493
832-404-4444

To Parrots With Love
Houston, TX 77064
713-504-3525

Loriinae Exotics
Pearland, TX 77584
www.Loriinae.com

Virginia
KB's Exotic Birds
Suffolk, VA 23434
757-539-8883

Wisconsin
Roxanne's Birds
Milwaukee, WI 53208-2246
www.roxannesbirds.webs.com

Aviaries and Breeders in the United Kingdom

Birdtrek
Helping Birdkeepers Since 2001
www.birdtrek.co.uk

Preloved
www.preloved.co.uk

Bird Trader
www.birdtrader.co.uk

Birds4Sale
www.birds4sale.co.uk

Parrot-Link
www.parrot-link.co.uk

UK Lories
www.uklories.co.uk

Lorikeet Buying Tips

You'll be more successful in acquiring a healthy bird from an aviary, but not all such facilities are created equal. When you visit an aviary to inquire about a bird, take a quiet assessment of the quality of the environment. It should be clean, light and obviously well maintained.

The birds themselves may be stressed if you approach them without warning. Just stand back and watch. The Lorikeets should be bright, happy, active and engaged. Birds that are sitting off by themselves, with or without feathers fluffed or who are disengaged may well be ill.

The bird's facial feathers should be completely free of discharge. If some matting is present, that could just be from their diet of nectar, but vomit is a bad sign. Also make sure that the area under the tail, the vent, is clean.

Ask to handle the bird, or ask the breeder to hold the bird for you, so you can examine the "keel" or chest. If you can feel the bone, the bird is too thin.

Even if you are confident a Lorikeet is happy and healthy, don't complete an adoption until a qualified avian veterinarian has passed on the animal's health and overall condition. Good breeders encourage such examinations. If the breeder with whom you are dealing balks at the idea, go to another aviary.

Rainbow Lorikeets and Children

Although Lorikeets are sweet, affectionate birds, they are not an appropriate pet to place in the care of a child. They simply require too much work and present too great a responsibility.

If you are bringing the bird into the home with the realistic expectation that you will be responsible for its complete care, then that is a different matter.

Certainly you can involve your children in keeping a Lorikeet, but don't let them handle the bird until they have been taught to do so properly and with kindness.

Lorikeets, like all companion animals, will retaliate when they're frightened or have been hurt. In most of these cases you have to ask yourself who is really at fault, the bird or the child?

Rainbow Lorikeets and Other Pets

As long as the proper precautions are observed to keep potentially dangerous interactions from occurring,

Lorikeets do fine with other pets. In fact, if there is trouble, you'd do well to assume the bird started it!

Dogs, for the most part, will just do a lot of looking through the cage, although pet Lorikeets have been known to taunt dogs. If that happens, and since it's really rather difficult to discipline a bird, just separate the two and give the Lorikeet a "time out" by covering its cage.

Don't ever yell at a vocal bird like a Rainbow Lorikeet. They'll just yell back, then the dog will start in barking, and you'll have a real mess on your hands.

You can go online and find videos of Lorikeets physically interacting with cats. Any such cross-species encounter depends entirely on the personalities of the individuals involved. Don't ever let such meetings go unsupervised. A cat is, after all, a cat . . . and a Lorikeet is a bird. Tragedy can ensue.

That being said, some Lorikeets form fast friendships with dogs, cats, and any other animals in the household. Just always remember that Lorikeets tend to completely over-estimate themselves and they have zero regard for danger in relation to their size. They think they can do anything, which can get them into trouble with other animals.

My best advice is not to take any chances but ultimately you must make a judgment call as you are best placed to know the character of your pets.

What About Wing Clipping?

First time parrot owners will encounter a great deal of conflicting advice on the controversial subject of clipping a companion bird's wings to prevent escape.

The traditionalist line of thinking holds that the procedure is for the bird's own good, and nervous new aviculturists sometimes think they can't control a parrot that is fully capable of flying away. Customarily, it has been done as a precaution against accidents that occur when the bird becomes startled and gets away from a nervous, new owner.

Young birds can be rambunctious. If they fly into windows or mirrors, they can injure themselves. So, although theoretically done in the name of protecting the bird, wing clipping is really a matter of convenience for the owner.

It might help to think of clipping back their flight feathers as inhumane as removing a cat's claws or clipping a dog's vocal chords to stop problem barking. The truth is that wing clipping is of much greater benefit to the bird owner than to the bird.

Young birds with clipped wings never become good at flying, even if the feathers are allowed to grow back. They never have the chance to develop strong chest muscles. In either case, the clipping has removed the bird's most essential defense mechanism — the ability to escape harm by taking flight.

If wing clipping is performed inappropriately, the Lorikeet can be injured severely enough to bleed to death. The risks and long-term consequences far outweigh any short-term benefits.

If you adopt a bird, you must learn how to handle the creature inside and outside the cage. Lorikeets are easily taught to get onto a perch with a command like "step up." Many aviculturists say that if you teach your bird nothing else teach him to "step up".

Then, if the bird is sitting atop the drapes, or the Christmas tree, or any other unreachable spot, you can extend a long-handled retrieval perch and ask the bird to "step up." Once he's onboard, just bring him back down to your level slowly.

A retrieval perch is nothing more than a long wooden dowel with a smaller dowel on the end set at a 90 degree angle. You can buy all the necessary materials at your local hardware store and build your own. Just drill a hole in the side of the long dowel, and glue the shorter piece into it. Total cost: less than $10 (£6.50).

The point is that all the "problems" associated with the very real necessity of free flight time for your bird can be addressed. Windows and mirrors can be covered. Netting can be put up to prevent escapes. As part of the process of getting to know your Lorikeet, you have to learn to safely handle the bird, including the times that it is out of the cage.

If you are going to have a pet bird, these experiences are part of the deal; wing clipping isn't and shouldn't be. It's cruel and unnecessary.

While wing clipping has long been a control measure with companion birds, it presents a true moral dilemma for bird owners and should be avoided.

Introducing a Second Lorikeet to the Household

If Lorikeets are kept indoors in a cage, they should be housed separately unless you are trying to keep a breeding pair (See Chapter 8 - Breeding Rainbow Lorikeets for more information).

Lorikeets are known for their territorial aggression. Simply put, one cage is just not big enough for two birds if they decide to start cordoning off what belongs to whom.

Certainly you can keep two Lorikeets in separate cages and they will likely do well. Free flight time, however, may not go as well. Remember that these are intelligent creatures with distinct personalities. It's difficult to predict what any one bird will do.

However, since most Lorikeets do develop very deep bonds with their owners, your bird will likely be very jealous if another bird is brought into the household. The result will not only be aggression toward the second Lorikeet but likely toward you as well!

Finally, these birds make a big mess. Their liquid feces must be cleaned up daily. Lorikeets are very high maintenance pets, and few people have the stamina to keep up with more than one cage daily.

Rainbow Lorikeets and Other Bird Species

If you have other species of birds, don't put the Rainbow Lorikeet in with them. People who keep multiple species of birds, which is generally in outdoor aviaries, must have a close understanding of "flock dynamics."

Lorikeets are highly territorial birds, and they can be aggressive to other birds of their own or another species. If space permits, then the different species can be kept segregated in the aviary until they get used to one another and then be introduced slowly.

Be aware, however, that this may not work and never lose sight of the fact that bigger birds will kill smaller ones.

Time Away from Your Lorikeet

All pet owners face one common concern: What happens when it is time to go on vacation? Many people travel with their pets, but the fact is pets cannot always go with their families. What will you do with your bird when you have to go away from home – on vacation or out of town for business or for a funeral, for example?

Consider who will watch your bird before the need ever arises. You have several options. Perhaps a friend or a family member, who has been around your bird and feels comfortable, can bring him home to care for him.

Pet sitters are also a popular option, especially in the United States where pet sitting businesses must be licensed and insured to operate. A pet sitter generally comes to your home to visit your pet – to ensure he has food, water and time out to exercise. Pet sitters typically charge per visit, and you can schedule several visits each day.

Is a pet sitter a viable option for your bird? That depends. How long will you be gone? Can you afford to have the pet sitter come several times each day to ensure your bird will get time out of his cage? Be sure, if you look for a pet sitter, to find someone who has experience caring for birds or who is willing to take the time to learn about Lorikeets and their care.

Before you hire a pet sitter or agree to a visiting schedule, the pet sitter will generally come to your home for an initial consultation. During that meeting, you will talk with the pet sitter about your bird, his schedule, his diet, and how often he requires a visit each day. But, more importantly, the meeting will allow your bird and the pet sitter to meet and to become comfortable around each other. Some pet sitters charge for this initial meeting but many do not.

You can find pet sitters in the United States through the National Association of Pet Sitters (www.petsitters.org) and Pet Sitters International (www.petsit.com). A comprehensive list of pet sitters in the United Kingdom can be found through the National Association of Registered

Pet Sitters (www.dogsit.com) and yes, they look after more than dogs!

Make sure that your pet sitter is insured and fully referenced as they will have access to you home and your pet. You should also contact your home insurance providers to confirm your cover is not affected by having a pet sitter stay at your home.

If you do not like the idea of a pet sitter, consider contacting your local parrot or large bird rescue. Some rescue organizations offer boarding and pet sitting services while others may just be able to provide you with recommendations of sitters.

The Parrot Society of the UK – or local bird groups – may also have members who offer to pet sit Lorikeets while their owners are on vacation.

If you do the footwork – asking friends, investigating pet sitters, and talking with local bird groups – you should have little trouble finding a knowledgeable person to watch your bird for you.

Coming Home Again

How will your parrot react when you return home, especially if you have been gone a considerable period? Well, birds are like people, so do not be surprised if your beloved friend is angry with you for having left him. Just like people, he will need time to shed that anger.

Be gentle with your parrot, talking to him and treating him like normal, so he can become reassured that everything is okay. Do not become overly aggressive with him or push him to adjust to his normal life. Doing so could backfire, and your bird may need even more time to get back to normal.

Pros and Cons of Owning a Rainbow Lorikeet

Rainbow Lorikeets have absolutely endearing and comical personalities. They're just fun to have around the house, hanging upside down and observing every detail of their surroundings with those bright, intelligent eyes.

They are intensely loyal, usually singling out a human "mate" and showering that person with their attention and devotion. Especially if a Rainbow Lorikeet has been hand-raised, you will have a friend for life, which with his lifespan translates to possibly 30 years.

Lorikeets are receptive to training. They can be taught to speak, although they are not especially well known for that trait. But they are so smart, many owners do successfully get them to "go" in a litter box — which is great if you can pull it off.

As I have mentioned, the biggest downside of owning a Rainbow Lorikeet is the mess. Their feces are not only wet and liquid, but they defecate at a 45 degree angle and seem intent on painting any adjacent surface. Some kind of skirting around the bottom of the cage is a must with this species.

If you have a Rainbow Lorikeet, you will need to clean the cage daily without fail. That means you will have to have a bird sitter willing to do the same if you're going to be away from home on vacation or for business. These are not low maintenance birds. It's essential you understand that from the beginning.

Chapter 4: Daily Care

Your first consideration in bringing a Rainbow Lorikeet home is to provide a suitable habitat for your new companion. Remember that these birds will attain a full-grown size of 10 to 15inches (25.4 to 38.1 centimeters).

With companion birds, the bigger the cage the better. In general, cages that are wide and long are a better choice than those that are tall and narrow, or that have a novelty shape. Round cages may look attractive but they actually provide less space for the bird to move around.

Lorikeets, like all parrots, like to have a corner to back into, and they enjoy climbing, so you'll want a cage with horizontal bars rather than vertical. Your bird will need to be in a central location in the house where there's lots of activity, but the cage should be against a wall to give him a better sense of security.

This is not just an issue of buying a cage, sticking the Lorikeet in it, and randomly placing the habitat. Your Lorikeet will need many items that, working together, provide a healthy, intellectually stimulating environment. Get ready to go shopping!

Shopping for Your Rainbow Lorikeet

The following list is intended to facilitate setting up a good "beginner's" habitat for your Rainbow Lorikeet. As you start to understand your bird's personality and individual needs, work to cater his environment to the things he likes and finds stimulating.

Cage

Rainbow Lorikeets are very agile birds and more active than most parrots. They are expert climbers, and they love to hang on the sides of their cages. Like most small to medium-range parrots, they will do best in "flight" cages or those that are rated as a suitable size for cockatiels.

The point is that your bird should be able to turn easily, flap his wings, hop from perch to perch, climb and play with only minimal limitations. Lorikeets need time outside their cages to free fly, but when they're in their "rooms" they need to feel both safe and as unrestricted as possible.

You may actually want to think outside the box when it comes to your Rainbow Lorikeet's home. Some owners use rabbit or ferret cages and others opt for large size wire dog kennels.

Regardless of the kind of cage you decide to buy, get horizontal bars, and make sure they are placed at a width of no more than 0.5 inch (1.27 centimeters). Anything wider and you run the risk of your Lorikeet getting his head stuck and potentially injuring or killing himself.

In terms of materials, look for a suitable cage that is made of stainless steel and hard plastics that are BPA free. Avoid antique cages and wooden cages. They may look great, but they aren't durable and wood in particular will harbor harmful bacteria. Remember, Lorikeets are highly susceptible to bacterial and yeast infections.

As an absolute minimum, look for a cage that is:

- 36 inches long (91.4 centimeters)
- 24 inches deep (61 centimeters)
- 48 inches high (122 centimeters)

If you're going to "splurge" on one luxury item for your bird, go with the biggest cage you can afford and comfortably fit into your living space.

As a point of price comparison, www.DrsFosterSmith.com offers a cage on a wheeled stand that comes with four food cups and two birch wood perches at a price of $250 (£162.50). The dimensions are 42 inches x 32 inches x 68 inches (107 centimeters x 81.3 centimeters x 173 centimeters).

Cage Skirts and Newspapers

Please remember that you will also want to investigate some kind of skirt or guard to place on the lower portion of the cage to minimize the amount of excrement that falls on the floor or adheres to nearby surfaces.

However, since many of these units are actually designed to catch seeds, and are made of sheer mesh, many Lorikeet owners simply wrap the bottom of the cage securely with common kitchen plastic wrap. If you go this route, just be certain there are no loose ends that might attract your bird's attention and lead to chewing. Also ensure that any plastic is PVC free.

You will also want to cover the floor under the cage with newspaper to catch the "fall out."

Make no mistake, Lorikeets are messy. These components of the cage will need to be switched out daily, so find the low cost, safe option that works for you and your bird.

If Possible Create an Outdoor Space

In the best of all possible worlds, no companion bird has to spend the majority of its time in a cage, especially a species like the Rainbow Lorikeet. If it is possible for you to do so, create an outdoor enclosure for your pet that will give the bird the maximum amount of freedom he can enjoy while remaining safe from the elements and from predators.

When it comes to size and form factors, outdoor aviaries are limited only by your budget and imagination. The same precautions apply for safety measures like bar spacing and material choices although wood does work outside so long as the aviary is well ventilated and can dry quickly and thoroughly. Should you choose wood, ensure that any weather proofing is non-toxic in case your bird chews the bars.

"Do it yourself" types routinely create spectacular environments for their companion birds. There are numerous plans available online, and photos to give you some ideas. If you are not "handy," work with a contractor to get an idea of the cost involved and what is possible in terms of available space.

Remember that any time you transfer a companion bird from an indoor to an outdoor space the bird should be securely transported in a carrier. Do not release a bird into an aviary unless there is absolutely no chance that your pet can escape.

Many aviaries feature a double door arrangement. You enter with your bird in its carrier, close the first door behind you, then enter a second door into the enclosure space proper. Working in this way, an open door does not become an invitation for a sudden and daring escape.

Ladders and Swings

Cage implements like swings and ladders are a great way to encourage your Rainbow Lorikeet to climb and perch. Many of these units are also outfitted with toys to accommodate a Lorikeet's natural and vigorous tendency to chew.

Cost: $5 to $15 (£3.25 to £9.75) each.

A Good Variety of Perches

Remember that in designing and outfitting a cage, you are trying to create as natural an environment as possible for the bird's habits and talents. Think of perches as the "branches" of your Lorikeet's personal tree.

Get as many perches as the cage can comfortably hold, picking a variety of sizes and style. Don't buy perches that are covered in sandpaper, as these can irritate your bird's feet to the point of causing open sores.

Cost: $5 to $15 (£3.25 to £9.75) each.

Intellectual Stimulation

We like to call the various points of interest in a bird's cage "toys," but remember that in the wild, these birds are foragers. They spend their days looking for food.

The "toys" you give your Rainbow Lorikeet are, for him, a replacement for the "work" he'd be doing if he were living on his own.

Lorikeets are very vigorous chewers and highly efficient shredders. You'll be replacing his toys often, so go for variety and ensure they are BPA and PVC free and non-toxic. Keeping your bird interested and engaged is vital for his physical and psychological health.

Cost: $4 to $15 (£2.60 to £9.75) each.

Nectar Mix, Treats and Vitamins

Do not feed your Rainbow Lorikeet seed or pellet diets. Many of these products make outrageous claims of controlling or "improving" the density of the bird's feces. Liquid feces are normal in this species. Constipation is NOT an "improvement."

You will want to purchase a good quality nectar mix for your bird, and supplement its diet with fresh fruits and vegetables. Dispense the nectar in the amounts recommended on the packaging and feed fresh fruits as the bird will consume them, removing uneaten fragments within a couple of hours.

Note: Lorikeets put fruit and vegetables in their beaks, squeeze out the juice, and spit out the pulp, so there will always be residue from fresh foods.

There is a wide variety of nectar mixes available for Lorikeets. Expect to pay approximately $7 to $10 per pound (£4.55 to £6.50) per 15.9 ounces / 0.45 kg.

As for treats, with Lorikeets it's best to use fresh fruit and vegetables. They are especially fond of grapes. The species is, as a whole, susceptible to nutritional diseases, so adhering to their natural diet as closely as possible is best for their overall health.

Some Lorikeet owners do use vitamin supplementation, but the use of these products can affect how the bird synthesizes iron in its diet.

Iron Storage Disease is a particular issue with Lorikeets, so use supplementation only under the guidance of your breeder or veterinarian and only as part of a broader consideration of the bird's diet. For more information on Iron Storage Disease, see Chapter 6 - Health.

Cuttlebone

All birds can be offered a cuttlebone as a toy for jaw exercise, a source of calcium, and a way to keep the beak worn down. The latter is especially important in a species like the Lorikeet that eats a soft diet.

Cuttlebones are the shells of Cuttlefish, and have a grainy texture like pumice. Some Lorikeets use them, others ignore them completely, but it doesn't hurt to offer your bird one in the beginning.

Cost: $1 (£0.65)

Mineral Block

Mineral blocks are also an option to provide your Rainbow Lorikeet with a source of calcium and a means to naturally wear down their beaks. As with cuttlebones, however, some Lorikeets take to them and others don't. Basically, it doesn't hurt to try.

Cost: $2 to $4 (£1.30 to £2.60)

Lava Stone

If your Lorikeet won't take a cuttlebone or a mineral block, you can try a lava stone for beak cleaning and trimming. Generally a bird will take to at least one of these offerings.

Cost: $5 (£3.25) for a stone measuring 2.5 inches x 2.5 inches x 1.25 inches (6.4 centimeters x 6.4 centimeters x 3.2 centimeters)

Food and Water Dishes

The largely liquid nature of a Lorikeet's diet makes it possible to feed these birds with simple cups that hang on the side of the cage. These work equally well to hold chunks of fresh fruit and vegetables.

Cost: $2 (£1.30)

Some Lorikeets will use inverted bottles with a "lixit" tip, which is a ball bearing from which water can be licked. So long as there is a consistent supply of clean, chlorine-free drinking water, simply go with the option that your bird seems to favor.

Cost: "lixit" waterer, $15 (£9.75)

Bath

Like most birds, Rainbow Lorikeets love a good splash in the bath. Simply hang a small tub to the side of their cage, outfitted with a splash guard that sits against the bars, and your bird will take it from there.

Don't fill the bath too full however. In the wild, Lorikeets bathe in small accumulations of water they find in the trees. They'll be happier with just a shallow amount of water.

Cost: $6 - $10 (£3.90 - £6.50).

Rainbow Lorikeets also love to be misted. Any clean "spritzer" type bottle set to a light mist serves well for this purpose, but don't re-use a bottle in which any household chemical or other substance was originally packaged. You cannot be certain that all residues have been removed from previously used containers.

Travel Carrier

Any time you need to carry your bird outside of the house, whether that's to a backyard aviary or for a vet visit, you will need a secure means of confining the Lorikeet.

You will want a travel carrier or "travel cage" for this purpose. These units are also handy to temporarily confine the Lorikeet while you're cleaning its cage in case your little feathered supervisor is being entirely too "helpful."

Cost: $60 - $120 (£39 - £78).

You could also consider a specialist harness when taking your bird outside. Take advice from your breeder or veterinarian.

Arranging Your Rainbow Lorikeet's Home

The only hard and fast rule about arranging your Lorikeet's new home is that the food and water dishes be placed in such a way as to be safe from contamination from droppings.

Otherwise, arrange the elements of the cage to maximize space, encourage movement and to create intellectual stimulation.

Place the cage in an area that gets good light, but not direct sun, and that is well ventilated without subjecting the bird to a draft. Avoid putting the cage directly in front of glass doors or windows, since this makes temperature regulation difficult.

Lorikeets are tropical birds and prefer temperatures on the warm side. They will do well in a temperature range of 72 F - 84 F / 22.2 C - 28.9 C. If necessary, you can provide additional heat with a specialist lamp designed for this purpose and placed close to the cage.

Cover the bird at night both to give him privacy, and to ensure he stays warm.

Birds that sit with their feathers fluffed out for long periods of time are trying to tell you they're cold. If, however, the Lorikeet is holding its wings away from its body and panting, the temperature is too high.

Picking the Right Cage Location

In the wild, Rainbow Lorikeets live high up in trees. They will not enjoy a cage that is placed too low to the ground, which will force the bird into a constant state of vigilance.

Remember that the Lorikeet will likely see you as its "mate"and your family as its "flock". Put the cage in an area that gets a lot of traffic.

Lorikeets like to see what's going on and feel like they're part of the action. This will help the bird's socialization and provide additional intellectual stimulation.

Cleaning Your Lorikeet's Cage

You will need to clean your bird's cage daily, removing the cage liner and wiping away feces adhering to the sides of the cage or adjacent surfaces. While commercial lining papers are available, newspaper works perfectly well.

Some owners express a concern about using newspapers with colored inks, but since Lorikeets are perching and climbing birds, they shouldn't be spending any time on the bottom of the cage. I would however, recommend you simply use the black and white pages.

Do not use kitty litter in the bottom of the cage especially "clumping" litter. Some companion birds will eat the litter, a practice which can be fatal.

At least once a week, your cage cleaning routine should include washing all parts of the enclosure with warm, soapy water. Also, disinfect all surfaces including perches and toys. Ensure that all soap and disinfectant residue is washed off. Do not return the bird to its habitat until everything has dried out thoroughly.

Once a month, take the cage apart completely and take it outside to be hosed down (or put it in the bath tub). Use natural disinfectants like vinegar and baking soda. Don't use household chemicals, which can be toxic to your pet.

Again, make sure all residue is removed for the cage and all its components, and allow everything to dry and air out before putting the Lorikeet back inside.

Handling Your Rainbow Lorikeet

Daily handling is an important part of keeping a Rainbow Lorikeet socialized. Since these are affectionate, gregarious birds, they are very receptive to being handled and typically only show aggression when they are going through the "terrible twos."

If you are dealing with a bird experiencing hormonal aggression, patience is the only answer. If you ostracize the bird for nipping and being unpleasant, its level of socialization will decline.

Remember, your parents were patient when you were a teenager. Try to give the bird the same consideration. The behavior will pass.

In handling a Rainbow Lorikeet or any bird, remember the basics.

- Avoid loud noises and quick, jerky movements.

- Speak softly and slowly.

- Under no circumstances should you ever shake the cage.

- Teach the bird the "step up" command to encourage perching.

- Create a routine, which makes the Lorikeet feel secure.

- Allow the bird time by itself. Even social Lorikeets need privacy.

Never grab a bird, or hold it so tightly it feels as if it's being squeezed. This is a terrifying experience for a Lorikeet.

Instead, place your palm lightly on the Lorikeet's back and gently place your fingers around the bird with your thumb and forefinger on either side of its head when you need to pick your pet up. Be gentle and slow and always speak reassuringly.

Don't overreact if your Lorikeet nips at you. The bites are more startling than serious. It's important that you be calm with your pet. The more loving and attentive you are, the gentler and more affectionate the Lorikeet will be in response.

Can Rainbow Lorikeets Talk?

The more accurate question might be, will Rainbow Lorikeets talk? Like all parrots, Lorikeets are capable of mimicking human speech, but they are not known as good talkers. If you want a parrot specifically for its verbal abilities, consider an African Grey, a Quaker or a Parakeet.

That being said, Rainbow Lorikeets, like all birds, learn from imitation. They love to be spoken to, and they will respond to verbal cues. They are quite capable of learning commands and engaging in "tricks."

Generally the best way to do this is to encourage some behavior in which the bird is already engaging and then try to build on it. Never try to force a Rainbow Lorikeet or any pet to "perform." If the animal is not interested and enjoying themselves, they won't do what you want and will likely become annoyed and aggressive.

Lorikeets are very playful and comical. Most owners agree that their birds "tricks" evolved naturally from play, so just have a good time with your bird. Learn what interests him and the things to which he responds and let his native behavior dictate any "lesson."

If you would like more information on teaching him further, then have a look at this informative video, "How to teach a bird to talk, a step by step tutorial" http://www.youtube.com/watch?v=o3oE_8EJa-E

"Potty" Training a Lorikeet

It is a matter of considerable debate as to whether a Rainbow Lorikeet can be trained to use a "litter box" or not. It's certainly possible to go on YouTube and watch videos of owners who claim success at potty training their pets.

These videos describe methods that, in theory, work, but remember, all Rainbow Lorikeets are individuals.

A word to the wise; be aware some of these videos use explicit language in regard to feces and defecation.

One thing is for certain, Lorikeets do respond to language. If you can get the bird to associate a verbal command with the act of defecation and positively reinforce this action with a treat, it is clearly possible to get a Lorikeet to "go" on command.

One method is to use a long shallow basket lined with newspaper that has a central arching handle that will serve as a perch. When the bird is settled on the handle, give the command to "go" and if the bird complies, reward it. In time, it is possible the Lorikeet will come to associate the basket as a place to do its "business," but it will want its treat as well.

Since runny Lorikeet stools are the principal maintenance issue with this species, it certainly won't hurt to try to get your bird to defecate in a designated spot, but be prepared for the process to require a great deal of patience on your part. If you decide to bring a Lorikeet into your life, please don't assume that you will be able to successfully 'potty train' him. There are no guarantees!

Free Flying Time

Rainbow Lorikeets need a lot of free flying time outside of their cages. This means you will need a secure, bird safe room in your home where you don't mind cleaning up the feces that will inevitably be splattered about.

You will want to provide the bird with a shallow bath outside the cage and acceptable perches. One good solution that can also help in localizing droppings is to buy a couple of "playgrounds" that will attract the bird's attention.

Playgrounds are simply edged trays or landing stations outfitted with perches, ladders and selections of toys. A typical unit would measure roughly 14.5 inches x 12.5 inches x 9.25 inches / 36.8 centimeters x 31.7 centimeters x 23.5 centimeters.

Cost: $20 (£13) per playground.

If at all possible, provide your Rainbow Lorikeet with access to a secure outdoor aviary. This will greatly minimize the cleanup for you, and maximize the bird's flight time and interest level.

Nap Time and Sleeping

Rainbow Lorikeets will get in several short naps during the day, a practice you can encourage by dimming the lights at a designated time and making the room quiet.

Expect your bird to sleep 10 to 12 hours a night, especially if you cover the cage. This is a good practice, as it gives the bird a sense of privacy and can keep the Lorikeet from waking you up at the crack of dawn.

Watch for Any Sign of Feather Plucking

In pretty much any species of companion bird, feather plucking is a clear message of either illness or unhappiness.

Often a Lorikeet that is not getting enough time with its human, or that does not have enough stimulation in its environment will pluck its own feathers.

Lorikeets also have a tendency to be aggressive with other birds, including their own kind, so missing feathers can also be a sign that aviary mates are fighting. Unless you are attempting to breed a pair of Lorikeets, the birds should be kept alone when caged.

If a Lorikeet is plucking its own feathers and the behavior does not improve with increased attention and environmental augmentation like more toys or perches, then consult with your veterinarian. Your pet may be ill.

Chapter 5: Quick Facts

L orikeets are the Broadway performers of the bird world. They put on quite a show, so it's much easier to learn their body language than with other, quieter species. Here's a "cheat sheet" for some of their most common "vocabulary."

Excitement

Rainbow Lorikeets who are excited will expand and contract their pupils, bob their heads and arch their necks. They may fluff out their feathers and tap one foot.

Be watchful, however, it's a short step from excitement to aggression and Lorikeet bites can hurt! If you think your bird is getting over-stimulated, you need to give him a chance to calm down before excitement turns to anger.

Aggression

A Lorikeet that's shifting into an aggressive mode will give you a highly concentrated stare. The bird will sit absolutely still, but his feathers may be ruffled a little.

As his agitation mounts, his body will stretch up and arch, his pupils will begin to "flash," and you may begin to see tongue and beak movements.

Obviously if your bird gives you a sharp nip he's sending a clear signal he wants to be left alone. Listen to him!

If two males are trying to show who is dominant they'll stand chest to chest, each one trying to stretch taller than the other. They'll also glare into each other eyes, each daring the other to make a move.

Nervousness

By nature, Lorikeets don't tend to be either nervous or fearful. If, however, you approach the cage and the bird backs up, leans away or tries to fly, slow down and quietly retreat. Something has spooked your pet and you don't want to make it worse.

It's important not to have negative experiences with your Lorikeet. They are very social birds, but they also have good memories, and their ongoing socialization is dependent on a calm, stable, loving and trustful relationship with you and the other humans in their lives.

Relaxation

When Lorikeets are happy and engaged with the environment around them, they show no sign of disturbance when approached. They will often sit with one leg up, and will be actively taking in what's going on around them.

Chewing is a good sign that a Lorikeet is happy and interested. They investigate everything with their beaks and tongues, and most of the time they're upside down while they're doing it.

Don't panic or over-react if your Lorikeet gently nibbles at you with its beak. That's not a bite waiting to happen, it's just your bird checking you out.

Sleeping

Lorikeets like to sleep on horizontal perches or in nesting boxes. When they're on a perch, they stand on one leg with the other foot drawn up into their feathers, and they tuck their heads under their wings.

This is actually a very good indicator of health. Lorikeets that are sick sleep on both legs, likely because they don't feel stable on the perch.

If your bird is feeling really great about life, however, it will fall asleep in almost any position, including hanging from the cage or even lying on its back with its feet up in the air. That one will give you a fright the first time you see it!

You're just as likely, however, to find the bird on its tummy, or hanging on to the side of the cage with its beak taking a snooze. For that matter, if your Lorikeet is riding around on your shoulder, especially if you're wearing a nice warm sweater, it might just tuck in against your neck for a little nap.

Preening and Bathing

You'll want to make sure your Rainbow Lorikeet has both drinking water and a nice bathing dish, but don't be surprised if the happy-go-lucky bird mistakes one for the other. They do love to splash!

Your bird will also spend a lot of time preening to keep his feathers in perfect condition. If you are housing a mated pair, they will happily preen one another. Birds that are not grooming are not in good health.

Attention Displays

Make no mistake, Lorikeets love attention and they will ask for it in a variety of ways. This may manifest as a slight crouch, with wings slightly extended and fluttering a little. There may be a bit of bobbing as well, which is a request for a head scratch.

This same posture can be begging for food if it's accompanied by loud squawking and an open beak. The message is clearly, "How can you do this to me? I haven't eaten in DAYS." Lorikeets are more than capable of engaging in a little melodrama!

Vocalizations

Lorikeets might as well wear watches. Expect them to know your routine down to the minute, and to get excitable around mealtime.

They'll happily announce to you that they're awake first thing in the morning and wanting their breakfast, and they'll be just as enthusiastic when you get home from work at the end of the day.

If, however, your Rainbow Lorikeet is normally fairly quiet and suddenly starts a lot of vocalizations, you need to evaluate what's going on.

The sounds may indicate:

- Pain

- Distress

- An objection to change in the environment

- Loneliness

It's even possible your Lorikeet is trying to tell you something you need to know about your own world. These birds notice everything that goes on around them. If your pet gets fixated on something in the room or outside the window, trust his powers of observation and investigate.

Chapter 6: Health

Rainbow Lorikeets are unique among companion birds due to the specialized nature of their diet, which relies on nectar, fresh fruit and vegetables rather than seeds and nuts.

These birds are susceptible to nutrition-based illnesses, as well as a host of diseases to which all birds can be subject. The more you know about potential problems, the better able you will be to monitor your Lorikeet's health on a daily basis.

Finally, finding and working with an avian veterinarian is one of the most critical aspects of caring for your companion bird. Because birds can sicken and die quickly, having all the pieces of your Lorikeet's healthcare plan in place rather than reacting in the heat of the moment can make the difference between life and death for your pet.

Is My Rainbow Lorikeet Healthy?

While daily handling is an important aspect of keeping companion birds well socialized, it is also a vital aspect of preventive medicine. Keen observation of your bird's habits and physical condition will help you to make sure your Rainbow Lorikeet is both happy and healthy. Some things to look out for are:

- Rainbow Lorikeets are active, alert, and very interested. Your little guy should be busy all the time. These birds perch and climb constantly, and it's perfectly normal for them to be upside down since that is their favorite and most efficient feeding position in the wild.

- Always watch for signs of discharge around the bird's nares or nostrils. They are located on the small, exposed area of flesh above the beak called the "cere." The cere should always been clean and dry, but not flaking, crusting, or peeling.

- Also be on the alert for any discharge from the eyes. A Lorikeet's expression should always be alert and bright.

  Eyes that are dull and listless are a sure sign of illness.

- Birds' ears are generally hidden from sight under a fine layer of feathers. The two small holes are located toward the back of the head and are just behind the eyes. You should never be able to see the ears unless the bird is wet from having been bathed.

- Rainbow Lorikeets' feces are much wetter than those of other birds, and they defecate at a 45 degree angle. The vent, the area under the tail feathers, should be clean and dry, otherwise the bird may be suffering gastrointestinal distress.

- Overall, a Rainbow Lorikeet's plumage should be shiny and vibrant, alive with color, lying smoothly in place with a tight, neat pattern of layers.

- Always watch for any signs of discoloration, flaking, dryness or injury around the feet, legs and beak.

Deformations of the feet are not uncommon in birds that have been hatched in captivity. As long as these issues do not keep the bird from perching and climbing, they don't affect its ability to be a great companion or to live a healthy life.

Is My Rainbow Lorikeet Unhealthy?

If you observe any of the following behaviors in your bird, the Lorikeet may not be feeling well and might need veterinary care:

- Even busy Rainbow Lorikeets will take naps during the day. Especially if the cage is covered, they will sleep 10 to 12 hours at night. If your Lorikeet is clearly lethargic, sleeping a good bit of the day, or seeming "out of it," get the animal to a vet.

- Lorikeets are perching and climbing birds, even getting their drinking water from the trees in which they live. They are strong and agile, and they use up a lot of energy. If a Lorikeet is sitting on the bottom of the cage, it's a sign that he's physically too weak to perch.

- As a defense mechanism, birds fluff out their feathers when they're not feeling well so they look bigger than they are and less helpless. It's also a way for them to stay warmer. In either case, feather fluffing for extended periods of time means something is not right.

- With most birds, loose stools are a sign of illness. With Lorikeets, just the opposite is true. If your bird's stools begin to get too firm, or the bird is not defecating often, he is likely constipated. This is a real problem with Rainbow Lorikeets since many pet food companies sell foods designed to "solve" the species' poop "problem." The only problem lies with humans who object to cleaning up what a Lorikeet does naturally. Liquid stools are completely normal for a Lorikeet.

- Be on the lookout for any signs of discharge from either the eyes or the nose. Both are a clear symptom of avian illness.

Take note of any changes in your Lorikeet's normal behavior, including his appetite. The longer you and the bird make your home together, the better you will know one another.

If you think that something is wrong with your pet, it probably is. It's much better to be out the price of a precautionary visit to the vet than to let an illness progress untreated. Birds can sicken and die quickly if they do not receive appropriate medical care.

Common Health Problems in Rainbow Lorikeets

As a companion species, Lorikeets tend to suffer most from poor nutrition due to the specialized nature of their diets. They do not eat seeds or nuts, and must be fed nectar and fresh fruits and vegetables to thrive in captivity. Like all birds, however, they are susceptible to common avian illnesses including the following: -

Iron Storage Disease

Iron storage (or iron overload) disease is a problem in all fruit-eating birds including Lorikeets, Mynahs and Toucans as well as Quaker Parrots. The principal symptoms are a loss of balance, weakness, lethargy and a depressed appetite.

There is some evidence that the disease may be hereditary, but it is most often seen in birds that are being fed fortified seeds and pellets rather than the fruits and vegetables they actually require. This leads to iron overload in the bird's diet.

The disease may also be caused by a genetic abnormality that results in the increased absorption of iron in the intestine, in which case it is called hereditary haemochromatosis.

Regardless of the cause, however, the bird's liver and other organs begin to store a toxic excess of iron. Fluids start to accumulate in the body, causing respiratory distress and congestive heart problems.

Since iron storage disease is not found in wild bird flocks, it is exclusively a health issue in captive birds and directly linked to inappropriate nutrition.

Adjustments to diet with the administration of supplements like copper or tannin to offset the iron overload are the standard treatments, with some alternative veterinarians advocating the use of green tea extract to prevent liver failure.

Aspergillosis

Aspergillosis is a respiratory disease caused by a fungus. It is rarely diagnosed until the bird is already extremely ill, and in most cases the vet is only making a speculative diagnosis based on white cell counts obtained from blood testing.

Typically aspergillosis is only a problem in birds that are kept in poor conditions. The fungus that causes the condition cannot thrive in cages and aviaries that are well ventilated, clean and well lit.

Since aspergillosis can present in combination with secondary bacterial infections, all treatments are tailored for individual birds. Always seek the aid of a veterinarian if your bird is lethargic, shows a depressed appetite and has discharge from the nostrils or eyes.

If any respiratory infection progresses to pneumonia, it's quite common for birds to go into shock and die.

Pacheco's Disease

Both parrots and lorikeets can contract Pacheco's Disease from any one of several strains of the herpes virus. The pathogens spread via direct contact with feces, contaminated food and water or as an airborne aerosol. Sadly, the illness is rarely detected until it is too far advanced to be treatable.

The primary damage is to the kidneys, liver and spleen. Symptoms present with discolored green feces, diarrhea, depressed appetite, lethargic behavior, trembling, ruffled feathers and red eyes.

If a Rainbow Lorikeet does survive a bout with Pacheco's, the bird will be a carrier for life and can never be housed with other birds again. For this reason, euthanasia is often considered the best course of action.

Pacheco's is a complicated disease and misunderstood because it is caused by one of approximately 130 strains of the herpes virus.

This family of viruses is responsible for varying diseases in many species, including humans where it is linked to chicken pox, cold sores, shingles, genital herpes, mononucleosis and Epstein-Barr.

While some herpes viruses are zoonotic, meaning they can pass between humans and animals, the viruses that cause Pacheco's Disease are not among them.

The virus occurs naturally in various bird species and spreads only from a carrier bird to a new host. It is completely possible for a bird to carry one of the herpes viruses for life and never become ill or infect another animal.

Chlamydiosis

Lorikeets have low natural resistance to chlamydiosis, also known as psittacosis, and are thus highly susceptible to infection. The disease is zoonotic and can therefore be transferred to humans.

On an annual basis in the United States, for instance, there are 100 to 200 reported cases of chlamydiosis in humans who keep some form of parrots, parakeets or budgerigars.

Many species of birds including pigeons, doves, cockatiels, cockatoos and budgies do have a high natural resistance to infection, but are carriers of the chlamydophila psittaci bacteria.

Susceptible species contract the disease when they inhale dust created by dried nasal secretions and fecal matter, often in circumstances where many birds are housed together. Humans contract the illness in the same fashion.

Since the organism can live for long periods of time outside the body even in dust form, it is highly contagious. Extreme caution must be taken when cleaning the cages of infected birds since it is so easy to distribute the dust and thus the pathogen.

In birds symptoms will include a depressed appetite with accompanying weight loss and dehydration. The Lorikeet will have discharge from both the nose and eyes and greenish stools. The bird will spend a great amount of time sitting lethargically with its feathers fluffed.

It is imperative that treatment be administered immediately. The most common course of action is oral or injected doxycycline over a period of 45 days.

If the bird survives, it must be re-tested a month later to determine its status as a carrier. During this entire time, the Lorikeet must be kept in isolation.

Humans with chlamydiosis will experience flu like symptoms of "Parrot Fever." If treatment is not sought, 15- to 20% of cases prove fatal.

Consequently, chlamydiosis or psittacosis must be reported to the U.S. Department of Agriculture and/or the local public health department and to the Department of Health in the UK.

Scaly Face and Leg Disease

Like all birds, Rainbow Lorikeets are susceptible to infestations of mites, which manifest as Scaly Face and Leg Disease.

If your bird has white deposits around the beak and eyes or on the legs and feet, the parasites are present and must be treated with oral or injected medications.

Never let an infestation of mites go untreated since long-term exposure to the parasites is not only extremely uncomfortable for the bird, but can lead to deformities of the legs and beak.

Feather Plucking

Any time a Rainbow Lorikeet begins to pluck its own feathers, the animal may be in either physical or emotional distress. It is natural for a few feathers to come out during the bird's routine self-grooming, but bald patches or bleeding areas are not normal and should be examined by a veterinarian.

Loss of feathers can be linked to all of the following conditions:

- Parasitical activity, primarily mites.

- An allergic reaction to something in the bird's environment.

- Liver disease including iron storage disease.

- Skin irritation, inflammation, or dryness.

- Nutritional deficiencies.

- Improper lighting and ventilation.

The Lorikeet may also be suffering from a lack of attention and intellectual stimulation. If, however, spending more time with the bird or enriching its environment does not stop the feather plucking, seek the aid of a veterinarian, especially if the bird is not eating or seems to be losing weight.

Caged Rainbow Lorikeets are best housed alone, but if your bird lives in an aviary with other Lorikeets or with birds of other species, missing feathers can be a sign of aggression.

Lorikeets are highly territorial, so aggression should always be considered under these circumstances.

Bacterial and Yeast Contamination

Lorikeets are susceptible to bacterial and yeast infections due to contamination of their water and food sources. It is recommended that a water cleanser be used at least once a week.

These preparations do not harm the bird in any way, nor do they have a negative effect on its gut flora which are tiny microorganisms within the digestive tract. Read all precautions on the product label, however, as many cannot be mixed with products designed to control parasites, with dietary probiotics or with antibiotics.

As an example, Vetafarm Aviclens Water Treatment is sold in 250ml bottles for approximately $17 (£11.05). It is administered in 5ml doses per 10 liters of drinking water with recommended water changes every 2 days in warm weather and every 3 to 4 days in cooler months.

Candidiasis

Of the potential yeast infections to which Rainbow Lorikeets are susceptible, candidiasis tops the list. When the bird develops white lesions around the mouth and throat and mites have been ruled out, candidiasis is the likely culprit.

The infection is caused by overgrowth of yeast in the digestive tract and presents with loss of appetite and instances of vomiting. The bird's crop may also be slow to empty and appear to be swollen.

The standard treatment for candidiasis is any one of several anti-fungal medications that can be obtained from your veterinarian.

Can Humans Be Allergic to Birds?

When a human being is allergic to any type of companion animal, the source of the irritation is "dander" or "dust." In cats, for instance, the protein Fel d 1 is present in the animal's saliva and sebaceous glands. When cats groom, saliva dries on their fur and flakes off in the environment causing an allergic reaction in sensitive humans.

Birds of all kinds, including Rainbow Lorikeets, create a great deal of dust when they preen, flap their wings or defecate. Since Lorikeets have much more liquid feces, this problem is somewhat mitigated by the need to clean their cages daily, but if the feces are allowed to dry, the resulting dust can easily be widely dispersed. In order to help alleviate this problem, many bird owners successfully manage the presence of dander in their homes by using a vacuum cleaner equipped with a HEPA filter. Please do your research carefully if buying one as the efficiency varies considerably from brand to brand.

Due to possible allergic reaction, it is often recommended that people who suffer from asthma not keep a companion bird. The triggered immune response to dander almost always involves respiratory distress, as well as itchy, watery eyes, skin irritations and rashes and sometimes acute respiratory distress.

An allergic reaction to one species does not, however, mean you are allergic to all animals. Unique proteins specific to each animal create the allergic reaction, so if you are sensitive to cats, you may be fine with a bird. The best option, however, is to be tested for bird allergies before you bring a Rainbow Lorikeet or any other species into your life.

Dander Pneumoconiosis

People who work intensely with birds of any kind and who live in close proximity to them will be subject to a much higher level of exposure to avian dander. This is particularly true for breeders or for those who keep large aviaries.

In these circumstances, it is possible to develop a respiratory condition called Dander Pneumoconiosis or Allergic Alveolitis, which damages the alveoli lining the lungs and thus reduces their operating capacity. However, clinical symptoms of this condition may not present for 10 to 20 years.

In its acute phase, pneumoconiosis causes a high fever, coughing, chills and severely labored breathing. The sub-acute form, however, is typically a dry cough that becomes increasingly persistent over time with gradual diminishment of lung capacity. For this reason, it's easy to ignore pneumoconiosis until the disease enters the more active stage.

If the exposure to high concentrations of bird dander continues, and if no precautions are taken to protect the lungs, permanent damage will result including severe and life threatening conditions like pulmonary fibrosis.

Bird Flu (Avian Influenza)

Although there has been a tremendous amount of frightening press about Bird Flu or Avian Influenza, it has not been found at this time to appear in companion birds like Rainbow Lorikeets.

However, it is only fair to point out that any bird can be infected with this virus, and transmission to humans is not only possible but probable.

The Bird Flu scare began in Asia, Europe and Africa in 2003. In these areas, various species were found to test positive for a deadly zoonotic form of the flu caused by the H5N1 Avian Influenza virus. Transmission typically occurs when humans encounter dried fecal matter produced by infected birds.

H5N1 is an emerging pathogen. Various global health agencies are actively monitoring its status, but presently the birds most affected are poultry raised in deplorable conditions at large facilities where the animals are densely packed together. There have also been some outbreaks in populations of aquatic species.

At the time of this writing, H5N1 is not considered an issue with companion birds but check with your vet regarding the current position before bringing a bird into your life. As noted previously, before making the decision to bring a companion bird into your life, we strongly recommend that you take advice from your doctor and veterinarian so that you have a full understanding of any risks to your own health.

Working with a Qualified Avian Veterinarian

Locating a veterinarian who specializes in the care of birds is one of the most important things you can do for your Rainbow Lorikeet.

Many small animal veterinarians simply have no experiences with the diseases and conditions common to companion birds.

If, however, it proves impossible to find an avian specialist in your area, you at least want to locate a vet open to learning about birds and who is willing to cultivate a long-term consulting relationship with an avian vet.

In the age of the Internet, such healthcare collaboration for the benefit of more exotic pets is much simpler and more common than in years past.

To begin your search for an avian veterinarian, consult:

- The Association of Avian Veterinarians (US) at www.AAV.org

- The European Association of Avian Veterinarians at www.EAAVonline.org

When you have narrowed your search to a potential number of candidates, schedule an office visit for no purpose other than meeting the doctor and discussing your pet.

Make it clear that you are coming to interview the vet, and that you have every intention of paying the customary office visit fee.

During your interview, there are some key bits of information you will want to discover, including, but not limited to:

- The number of years the doctor has been treating birds.

- His degree of familiarity with Rainbow Lorikeets.

- Veterinarian associations in which he holds membership.

- Whether or not the vet has himself owned birds.

- The availability of emergency services.

- An estimate of typical fees associated with avian care.

- A proposed schedule of checkups

Basically you are trying to get a sense of the vet's personality and of his commitment to working with birds. This is, after all, a person with whom you will be engaged in a partnership relationship with the goal of keeping your pet happy and healthy. It is always best to both like your veterinarian and trust his opinion and expertise.

Taking Your Bird to Meet the Vet

When you find an avian veterinarian with whom you are comfortable, set up a follow-up appointment that will include your Rainbow Lorikeet.

Not only will the vet need to make an initial wellness examination to establish benchmarks in the bird's medical records, but it's important to see how the vet and other staff members interact with the animal.

Lorikeets have distinct personalities, with clearly evident preferences. If your bird is not comfortable in the clinic environment, the arrangement is likely not going to work no matter how much you like the vet.

Do ask if the vet would consider working with the bird in your home. Some avian vets will do this considering birds do not always travel well, but be prepared for the additional expense of a house call.

Your goal is to have an easy relationship with your vet, one that will benefit both you and your bird. Anything less is not an optimum situation for any of the parties concerned.

Pet Insurance

Veterinary care, especially for birds, can become quite pricey. In addition to the fact that avian vets generally come with a higher price tag, you never know when an illness or injury will occur, resulting in expensive and unexpected costs.

With advances in veterinary care, today's pets can receive the same high quality care – such as chemotherapy for cancer and physical therapy for injuries – as their human counterparts. The cost of that care, however, can become quite hefty, making it essential for you to know how you plan to pay for veterinary care even before you bring your bird home.

Many pet owners have discovered that pet insurance helps defray the costs of veterinary expenses. Pet insurance is similar to health insurance in that you pay a monthly premium and a deductible and the pet insurance pays for whatever is covered in your plan, such as annual exams and blood work.

Shopping for pet insurance is similar to shopping for health insurance in the United States. As with health insurance, the age and the overall health of your Lorikeet will determine how much you will pay in premiums and deductibles. Ask plenty of questions to determine the best company and plan for your needs which should include:

- Can you go to your regular vet, or do you have to go to a vet assigned by the pet insurance company?

- What does the insurance plan cover? Does it cover annual exams? Surgery? Emergency illness and injury?

- Does coverage begin immediately?

- Are pre-existing conditions covered? In addition, if your Lorikeet develops a health issue and you later have to renew the policy, is that condition covered when you renew your policy?

- Is medication covered?

- Do you have to have pre-authorization before your pet receives treatment? What happens if your bird has the treatment without pre-authorization?

- Does the insurance policy cover dental issues and chronic health problems, including any allergies to which they may be prone?

- Is there a lifetime maximum benefit amount? If so, how much is that amount? A benefit plan with a lifetime maximum of only a few hundred dollars surely will not suffice for a Lorikeet (or most pets, for that matter).

- Is there an excess limit i.e. an amount that you have to pay before the insurance pays out?

Take the time to research your pet insurance options. Compare the different plans available, what each covers, and the cost before making the decision on which is best for you and your pet.

Pet insurance may not be the answer for everyone. While pet insurance may not be a feasible option for you, consider having a backup plan, just in case your bird requires emergency care or you run into unexpected veterinarian costs.

A simple way to prepare for an emergency is to start a veterinary fund for your Lorikeet. Decide to put a certain amount of money aside each week, month, or paycheck to use in the case of an emergency. Think about the potential financial costs of veterinary care and plan for how you will pay for it now instead of waiting until something happens.

Chapter 7: Care Sheet

With any species of companion bird, including Rainbow Lorikeets, it's important not to use cookware and appliances with non-stick surfaces in the same room as your pet, or potentially even in the same house. If these products overheat, they can release toxic fumes that may kill your bird.

Overview

Although Rainbow Lorikeets are cheerful, good-natured companions, they do require daily interaction to remain happy and socialized. Also, due to their nectar and fruit-based diet, their droppings are naturally liquid. It is essential that their cage be cleaned daily.

Housing

Rainbow Lorikeets need a lot of time outside of their cages to free fly. Be prepared to set up a bird safe room, or to provide your pet with a secure outdoor enclosure in addition to its indoor habitat.

The minimum size cage for this species is 36 inches long x 24 inches deep x 48 inches high / 91.4 centimeters x 61 centimeters x 122 centimeters. Be sure to purchase a unit with horizontal bars that are spaced at a width no greater than 0.5 inch (1.27 centimeters).

The cage should also be outfitted with a lower skirt or guard to help prevent bird droppings from splattering on adjacent surfaces.

Cage Placement

Wild Rainbow Lorikeets live high in the trees. In captivity, they do not like being housed close to the ground. Bring the cage up to at least your eye level.

Lorikeets are highly social. Position the cage in a room that gets lots of traffic. Put one side of the cage against a wall to give the bird a better sense of security. Do not put the cage directly in front of a window or in a draft.

Maintain a temperature of 72 to 84 F (22.2 to 28.9 C).

Cage Cleaning

Establish a daily, weekly and monthly routine of cage maintenance. Each day, you will want to change your Lorikeet's food and water, cleaning the dishes to ensure no bacteria or "scum" accumulates. Change the liner in the cage, and clean debris from the cage skirt.

Lorikeets need fresh fruit and vegetables to supplement their nectar-based diet. Since the birds will squeeze their food to remove the liquids and then spit out the pulp, always remove the "leftovers" within an hour or two of feeding.

Each week, wash and disinfect all cage elements with warm soapy water. Monthly, dismantle the cage and disinfect with vinegar and baking soda. Do not use cleaning chemicals and ensure any cleaning residue is thoroughly rinsed. Always allow all elements to dry thoroughly before putting the bird back inside its cage.

Transportation

Any time that your bird is taken out of the house, even on a short trip to your own backyard aviary, secure your pet in a travel cage or crate. Never release the bird until you are safely inside another structure with all windows and doors closed. You could also consider a specialist harness when taking your bird outside. Take advice from your breeder or veterinarian.

Cage Accessories

Rainbow Lorikeets are very busy birds. Supply your pet with a variety of ladders, swings, perches and hanging toys both for chewing and intellectual stimulation. Lorikeets are problem solvers and investigators by nature.

Food

Do not use seed or pellet diets with Rainbow Lorikeets. Your bird needs a good-quality nectar mix fed as a liquid or powder supplemented with fresh fruits and vegetables.

Cuttlebone, Mineral Block, Lava Stone

Each of these devices has the same primary purpose, to provide the bird with a means to wear down its beak. While cuttlebones and mineral blocks are a good source of calcium, not all Lorikeets will use them.

Any one or combination of these three items in addition to adequate chewing toys will keep your pet's beak in good condition.

Vitamins

With a well-balanced and species-appropriate diet, vitamin supplementation should not be necessary. Since Rainbow Lorikeets are prone to develop Iron Storage Disease, and supplements can alter how your pet synthesizes iron, only use vitamins on the advice of a qualified avian veterinarian.

Socialization

Rainbow Lorikeets are naturally affable and good-natured birds. They do, however, like a lot of interaction with their humans and need daily socialization to remain gentle and non-aggressive pets.

This is not just a matter of cage placement for intellectual stimulation. You need to play with, talk to and handle your

Lorikeet daily.

Water

Provide your bird with clean, de-chlorinated water at all times. This can be served in an open dish or an inverted bottle with a "lixit" ball bearing tip. Also give your Rainbow Lorikeet a larger bathing dish.

Don't be concerned if the bird confuses the purpose of the two dishes. Make sure both the drinking dish and the bath are de-chlorinated, clean and free of debris on a daily basis.

Signs of Illness

Rainbow Lorkieets have a rather disturbing habit of sleeping on their backs with their feet extended. Don't panic the first time you see this!

The birds will nap during the day. Don't be concerned unless they are napping all day, and doing so with both feet on their perches. A Lorikeet that is sleeping normally on its perch will have one leg drawn up and its head tucked under its wing.

Other potential signs of illness include discharge from the eyes or beak, coughing and wheezing, swelling around the eyes, loss of appetite, failure to groom, soiled feathers *or* sitting with the feathers fluffed out.

Chapter 8 – Breeding

Rainbow Lorikeets are an easy species of parrot to breed, reaching sexual maturity around 2 years of age. Since it is almost impossible to tell males and females apart, and if you are new to the business of breeding, you may want to buy a mated pair, or get help from an established breeder.

Many people who keep aviaries and raise birds professionally have their birds DNA tested to establish gender and band the individuals to ensure proper identification.

It is important to understand that Rainbow Lorikeets mate for life, so once a pair has established a bond, they should never be separated. Lorikeets that bond most successfully have been socialized with other Lorikeets in a community environment and are not completely dependent on humans for a sense of "flock."

Most Lorikeets that are sold as breeding stock have been raised by their parents rather than hand-raised for the same reason. A female Lorikeet will take very quickly to a nesting box and will generally lay no more than two eggs, which will incubate over a period of 23 days.

Reasons to Hand Rear Lorikeet Chicks

The decision to hand rear Lorikeet chicks is a trade-off of desired end results. Birds that are hand reared are highly socialized and make excellent pets, but they don't make good parents in the future, because they bond with their owner rather than another Lorikeet.

Reasons to hand rear chicks include:

- The parents reject the chicks and won't feed them.

- The parents are plucking the chicks' feathers.

- You want to raise the chicks to be tame pets.

- You want to increase the number of births per mating season.

There is also the fact that some people just want to have the experience of raising a baby bird. If you believe that's what you want to do, you need to understand the real nature of the responsibility you are assuming. It's no small job!

Regardless, anyone undertaking a breeding situation with a companion bird needs to be informed about the hand rearing process as it may become an emergency necessity with little or no warning.

Please note that the following information is intended as a broad overview only. It is strongly recommended that if you want to raise or breed Rainbow Lorikeet chicks, you seek the advice and mentorship of an established avian breeder.

Caring for Rainbow Lorikeet Chicks

Newly hatched Lorikeet chicks must be fed every two hours. If you are plunged into this responsibility, you need to have all the necessary supplies on hand. Having access to a qualified avian veterinarian or an experienced Lorikeet breeder who can help you and answer questions is a definite plus.

It is imperative that you use a non-toxic hand sanitizer before you touch the chicks. The babies are very delicate and fragile. They must be handled with infinite gentleness and care.

Within six hours of hatching, the chicks must be fed. If it is necessary to remove them from their parents' care, they must be housed in a brooder where the temperature is maintained at approximately 95 F to 98 F / 35 C to 36.7 C.

As the chicks age, the temperature in the brooder can be gradually decreased, usually by a degree or two per week. By the time the chicks are two months old, they should be comfortable at a room temperature somewhere in the range of 72 to 74 F / 22.2 to 23.3 C.

Observe the chicks' behavior. If they begin to pant, they are too warm and should be removed from the brooder temporarily. Reduce the temperature by one degree until the chicks again appear comfortable.

Chicks that are cold will tend to huddle together in the center of the unit, so the temperature in that circumstance should be raised a degree at a time.

Use a plastic pipette, syringe, or eyedropper to feed the chicks. All of these items are sold at a cost of approximately $1 (£0.65).

Any time you are breeding birds, have the supplies you need on hand well before the eggs hatch. You do not want to be caught on the weekend or at night with baby birds needing care you cannot deliver because you do not have the correct equipment.

What is a Brooder?

Don't be intimidated by the term "brooder." It's nothing more than a contained area to raise baby chicks where temperature can be regulated. Even a sturdy cardboard box will suit the purpose in a pinch. The most important thing is temperature regulation and ensuring there are no drafts.

You will definitely want a digital thermometer to monitor conditions. They are inexpensive, and can be acquired for $7 to $10 (£4.55 to £6.50).

You will need a heat source, generally a specialist heat lamp that is positioned over the box. A unit with a thermostat is ideal. (Be sure to have a second bulb in case the first one burns out). It doesn't matter if the bulb is clear or infrared.

For a heat lamp with a thermostat, expect to pay $35 to $50 (£22.75 to £32.50) with replacement bulbs selling for $10 to $15 (£6.50 to £9.75).

Hand Feeding Chicks

It is important never to force a baby bird to eat, and never to overfill its crop, which is a chamber situated between the esophagus and stomach. Food is held in the crop for partial digestion before moving downward.

The crop is clearly visible in baby chicks with no feathers and is an excellent indicator of how much and when to feed. As confirmed above, never overfill the crop, and don't feed the bird again until the crop is empty.

A baby chick's first meal should be an electrolyte solution like Pedialyte (US) or Oral Rehydration Solution (UK). This will ensure that the chick's digestive system is functioning correctly.

For the second and subsequent feedings use a commercial hand feeding formula prepared according to the directions on the packaging. Typically the solution will be made to a temperature of 105 F to 108 F / 40.6 C to 42.2 C.

Baby birds eat very tiny amounts in the beginning, only a couple of drops at a time.

Use the status of the crop as an indicator, but expect to need to feed the baby every two hours, just at the point when the crop is almost completely empty.

Gently place a single drop of the solution on the LEFT side of the chick's mouth when feeding. If the baby refuses, return it to the brooder and wait 15 minutes before trying again.

Hand Feeding Formula

One of the most widely used of all feeding formulas for baby birds is Kaytee Exact. It is well respected by professional breeders, and was the first "instant" formula on the market.

Always prepare the mixture STRICTLY according to the instructions.

Have the product on hand just in case. You'll pay $10 (£6.50) for 18 ounces / 0.51 kg.

If Kaytee is not available in your area, other infant formulas on the market are made by ZuPreem, LeFeber and inTune.

Note: The website maintained by the makers of Kaytee has an excellent video tutorial on hand feeding baby birds. The company's "Ask the Experts" section is also an excellent resource to understand more about hand feeding. See: www.kaytee.com/pet-birds/general-care/hand-feeding.htm

Weaning the Chicks

As baby birds mature, their crops will empty more slowly and they will require fewer feedings per day. When they are down to just a couple of hand feedings per day, most chicks begin to refuse their formula and they can be weaned onto a diet of adult food.

It's perfectly normal for fledglings to lose a little weight during this dietary transition. It can take a couple of weeks for the bird to begin to drink nectar and eat fruits on its own. Even on a single hand feeding per day during this period, your bird's nutritional needs will be met.

NEVER, under any circumstances, should you force-feed a baby bird.

To a large extent, in this period, you are grappling with a psychological dependency. The Lorikeet wants your attention, which it equates with being fed.

Continue to spend time interacting with your little pet and it will soon accept the different dietary approach and settle down to eating adult food.

Often Rainbow Lorikeets can be weaned at an earlier age than seed-eating birds. When you begin to offer them nectar for the first time, you can either use a shallow container into which you gently push their beaks as if teaching a puppy or kitten to drink or you can offer the baby a spoon.

The point is to get the fledgling to understand how to use his very well adapted brush tongue to take in his nourishment. Be patient. It may take the little one a few days to get the hang of things, but generally just a taste or two will cause the bird's instinct to kick in.

Leg Banding in Professional Aviaries

Typically breeders who raise Rainbow Lorikeets and other birds for sale put a leg band on hatchlings for identification purposes. The band will include:

- The breeder's initials

- The place of breeding

- Year of hatching

- Gender (if DNA testing has been conducted)

- A unique identification number

Many bird owners feel that leg bands are an irritation to their pet and a potential danger should they get caught on elements of the cage. It is imperative that you never try to remove a leg band from a companion bird without professional assistance. Specific tools are required. If you want a leg band taken off, see an avian vet, a professional breeder or seek help at a bird shop.

A Final Word on Breeding Rainbow Lorikeets

This chapter is intended only as a broad overview of breeding and raising Rainbow Lorikeet chicks. While these birds are easier than many species, this can still be a complicated and labor-intensive process and a heartbreaking one if the chicks don't survive.

For your sake and for that of the birds, you should set out to be completely over-prepared before undertaking the care of your first set of hatchlings. This is more than just having the necessary equipment on hand. You need to fully research the process, including talking or corresponding with breeders who have vast experience with Rainbow Lorikeets.

The tiny, fragile creatures that emerge from those eggs will depend on you entirely, especially if you intend to remove them from their parents' care. Even experienced breeders admit they can still find the process both daunting and exhausting.

Raising any baby animal can be a wonderfully rewarding experience, but never lose sight of the tremendous responsibility involved. It's not something to be undertaken lightly, and the more support resources at your disposal, the better.

Chapter 9: Life After You

Sometimes life takes unexpected turns. If you have ever volunteered at or have been to an animal shelter, you have likely heard the heartbreaking stories of some of the homeless dogs, cats, birds, rabbits and other animals. Their beloved human has passed away and they are now at the shelter, confused and depressed. Countless pets languish in animal shelters and rescues after their owner dies because the person failed to make plans for their pet's future without them.

Most people expect to outlive their pets by many years. But, that does not always happen. What will happen to your parrot once you are gone? Lorikeets have a much longer lifespan than most pets, so that is a question you really want to think about and answer now. If something happens to you, you want to know that your bird will be properly cared for and loved.

Some cell phones allow you to input an ICE (In Case of Emergency) number with notes. If your cell phone has such an option, I recommend that you use it. Alternatively, you might find it easier to write the following information on a piece of a paper and put it in your wallet with your driver's license. You can also give a copy of this information to your neighbors along with friends and family. The list should include:

- The names of each of your pets, including your Lorikeet.

- The names and phone numbers of family members or friends who have agreed to temporarily care for your pets in an emergency.

- The name and phone number of your avian veterinarian.

Be sure to also talk with your neighbors, letting them know how many pets you have and the type of pets. That way, if something happens to you, they can alert the authorities, ensuring your pets do not linger for days before they are found.

If you fail to do that and something happens to you, someone will find your pet and will have questions: What is his name? What does he eat? How old is he? To make sure your bird is not forgotten in the case of an emergency, ask several friends or family members to be responsible for taking care of him temporarily should something happen to you.

Even before something happens, prepare instructions for the intended temporary guardians, providing amended instructions as necessary. Also, if you are happy to do so, provide each individual with a key to your home. Remember to let your home insurer know you have done so and ask them to confirm that does not affect your coverage. Instructions should include:

- The name and phone numbers of each individual who agreed to temporarily take care of your parrot and other pets.

- Your Lorikeet's diet and feeding schedule, so he can maintain his normal schedule.

- The name and phone number of your avian veterinarian.

- Any health problems and medications your bird may take on a daily basis, including dosage instructions, instructions on how to give the medicine, and where the medicine is kept.

- Information on the care of your parrot, such as when he typically sleeps, how much time he generally gets out of the cage, and so on.

Put as much information as necessary to ensure the temporary guardians can provide the same level of care to which your Lorikeet is accustomed.

Finding a Permanent Home for Your Rainbow Lorikeet

Ensure your bird's future by finding a permanent home for him in case of your unexpected incapacity or death. Here are some things to keep in mind when considering a new home for your beloved friend in the event of your death:

- Consider family members and friends who love animals and have successfully cared for pets themselves. You may have a particular family member, for example, who is fond of your Lorikeet and vice-versa.

- How many pets do you have? If you have a pair of Lorikeets, do not split them up if at all possible.

Breaking up a pair could result in great distress, including self- mutilation, feather plucking and screaming.

- Is the person you are considering willing to care for a parrot, regardless of how long he lives? He may even outlive his new guardian.

- Find an alternate new guardian in case something happens and the first one is unable to care for your pet as intended.

Always remain in contact with the potential new guardian to ensure he or she is still able or willing to care for your bird (and other pets) in case of an emergency. If one person backs out, you can then take the time necessary to find another potentially permanent guardian.

Making it Legal

Once you have found the best caregiver, consult with a lawyer or a solicitor. The lawyer/solicitor can create a legal agreement, whether a will or a trust, that is based on what you want for your pet in the case of your unexpected death.

A will can dictate who your bird is to live with upon your death while you can place funds – to help pay for the ongoing care of your Rainbow Lorikeet – in a trust that the guardian can use to help care for him.

Another alternative is to take out a suitable life insurance policy which can be written under trust for your pet's guardian. This is a complex area and I recommend you take specialist advice.

While it is not the most pleasant topic to talk or to think about it, it is extremely important to your pet's continued well-being that you address what is to happen to him and who will take care of him before that time comes.

Chapter 10: Closing Thoughts

I t's almost impossible to look at a beautiful, bright-eyed Rainbow Lorikeet hanging impishly upside down in its cage without being taken instantly by these remarkable creatures.

To see a flock of Lorikeets playing and clowning together in a tree is to witness a scene of pure joy. Nature has made the Lorikeet a good-natured and happy creature, well adapted to his environment, and more than willing to share his life with us in exchange for good care and proper affection and attention.

Although not known as a talkative species of parrots, Rainbow Lorikeets are highly intelligent and love to interact with their humans. Once you understand their language, you will realize that these jewel-toned creatures express open affection and concern for their humans and are constantly observing and taking in information from their environment.

Intellectual stimulation and social interaction are vital for the health and well-being of a Rainbow Lorikeet. This is not a creature to be placed in a cage, fed and otherwise ignored. Try it, and you'll have one cranky bird on your hands that is perfectly capable of aggressively telling you just how unhappy he is.

Lorikeets also need time outside of their cages to free fly, which means at the very least a bird-safe room in your home, or, if circumstances permit, a large and secure outdoor aviary.

The principal thing that must be understood about companion Rainbow Lorikeets is the liquid nature of their feces. This is a natural consequence of their nectar and fruit-based diet, complicated by their 45-degree angle of defecation.

Their cages must be cleaned on a daily basis and should be

outfitted with some kind of skirt or guard. When your Lorikeet is out of the cage, he will "go." Some owners have been successful in teaching their birds to "go" in a designated basket or tray but there are no guarantees that you will be able to "potty" train your bird.

The younger you start this lesson the better, but either way, you are the one who will be cleaning up after your Lorikeet – daily. The cage will also need weekly and monthly cleanings. Don't think for one minute that a Rainbow Lorikeet is a low-maintenance pet.

But, if you are prepared to take all this on, and to give your bird the care and attention he needs and deserves, you will be welcoming a companion into your life that could be with you for the next 30 years.

Deciding to live with a Rainbow Lorikeet should not be a snap decision, but if your choice is informed and well considered, this is one of the most beloved of all companion birds.

Chapter 11: Frequently Asked Questions

What's the difference between a Lory and a Lorikeet?

The distinction is similar to that between a parrot and a parakeet. Birds with long, pointed tails are called "keets." The ones with the short, square tails are Lories. In Australia, both kinds are referred to as Lorikeets. Often these terms are used interchangeably.

Which Rainbow Lorikeets make the best pets?

There are many species of Lorikeets. The ones that are generally considered to be the best companion birds are Rainbows, Swainson's and Edward's.

Can I add a Rainbow Lorikeet into a flock with other parrots?

Mixing a Lorikeet into an existing flock should be done very carefully since this species can become aggressive. The best strategy is mix them with birds of a like size. If the Lorikeet is the larger bird, he may well take the chance to also be the bully.

Do Rainbow Lorikeets like to bathe?

Lorikeets do enjoy having a bath, but they all have their own favorite style of grooming. Some prefer to splash around in a shallow bowl, and will even enjoy being placed in the kitchen sink with an inch or two of water from time to time.

Other Lorikeets prefer just to rub up against something that is wet, like a plant that has been heavily misted with water.

Most individuals, however, if given their own bathing dish from an early age, will use that option.

I'm hand-feeding baby Rainbow Lorikeets and they're huddling together. Should I be worried?

Baby birds that are huddled together could be simply

propping one another up, which is normal, but they could also be cold. Observe their behavior and if the huddling continues or intensifies, increase the temperature in the brooder by a degree. Continue to watch the babies. If they begin to pant, they are too warm and the temperature should be adjusted back down.

Can I give my Rainbow Lorikeet flowers?

Flowers for a pet Lorikeet are fine as long as you know the source, and know that no systemic fertilizer has been used. The presence of chemicals could be toxic to your pet. As long as the flowers are free of chemicals, Lorikeets will enjoy: - hibiscus, eucalyptus, bottlebrush, meleluca, dandelion, roses and pansies. It is wise to check with your breeder before introducing flowers to your Lorikeet.

Are there any special precautions to be taken when a Lorikeet is free flying?

Obviously cover all windows and mirrors. Birds can mistake those items as exits through which they can fly and seriously harm themselves. It's important not to have any tangling hazards in the room, or anything on which the bird could chew that would prove harmful, like an unprotected electrical cord.

What is the correct size cage for a Rainbow Lorikeet?

All companion birds should have the largest cage you can afford and accommodate in your home. For a Rainbow Lorikeet, the minimum size would be 36 inches long (91.4

centimeters) x 24 inches deep (61 centimeters) x 48 inches high (122 centimeters).

Be sure to get a cage with horizontal bars that are spaced no more than 0.5 inch (1.27 centimeters).

Is it true that Rainbow Lorikeets should not be feed honey?

The only stipulation is to not feed raw honey, which can carry botulism. Pasteurized honey is fine as a treat.

Any suggestions on how to handle the mess Lorikeets make with their feces?

Always have a skirt or guard around the bottom of the cage and don't ever run out of newspaper! Controlling the feces when the bird is out of the cage is difficult. Some owners have successfully trained their birds to land in one spot to do their "business." Others simply make sure that everything in the room is either washable or covered in plastic. Get creative and do what works in your environment.

Where are Rainbow Lorikeets found in the wild?

In the wild, a total of 53 species of Lorikeets are found in Australia, New Guinea, Polynesia and have been introduced into New Zealand and Hong Kong. Some are endangered, but others are considered agricultural pests.

How long will my Rainbow Lorikeet live?

With proper care, a Rainbow Lorikeet could live to be 30 years old.

Will sunflower seeds hurt my Lorikeet?

A few sunflower seeds won't hurt your bird, especially if he likes them. The bulk of his diet, however, must be nectar, and the juices he derives from fresh fruits and vegetables. Lorikeets cannot thrive on a diet of seeds and nuts.

I understand Lorikeets have strange sleeping behaviors. What are they?

The most disturbing napping behavior a Rainbow Lorikeet displays is sleeping on the floor of his cage on his back with his feet sticking straight up. Needless to say, the first time an owner sees this, they assume the worst, but just gently call your bird, or touch him lightly and you'll likely be rewarded with an eye peeled open and an expression that says, "What?"

Most of the time, Lorikeets will sleep on their perches with one leg drawn up and their heads tucked under their wings. If a Lorikeet is sleeping with both legs down, he probably doesn't feel good. Some birds like to sleep in nesting boxes, and others will doze off clinging to the side of the cage with their beaks.

Chapter 12: Relevant Websites

W hen you start looking around the internet it can take some time to track down exactly what you are looking for.

A one-stop shop for all your parrot needs is what is required and the sites below offer you the convenience of pulling together many of the best products from around the web.

Shopping

United States of America Website

www.tropicalbirdshop.com

United Kingdom Website

www.tropicalbirdshop.co.uk

American Federation of Aviculture
www.afabirds.org

American Lory Society
www.lorysociety.com

AvianWeb
www.avianweb.com

Avicultural Society of America
www.asabirds.org

Aviculture Society of the United Kingdom
www.avisoc.co.uk

Bird Channel - The Website for Bird Lovers
www.birdchannel.com

Bird Talk Magazine
www.birdtalkmagazine.com

International Association of Avian Trainers and Educators
www.iaate.org

The Internet Bird Collection: Rainbow Lorrikeet
ibc.lynxeds.com/species/rainbow-Lorikeet-trichoglossus-haematodus

Loriinae Exotics
www.loriinae.com

Lorikeets
www.Lorikeets.com

Parrots Magazine
www.parrotmag.com/home

Parrot Rehabilitation Society
www.parrotsociety.org

Parrot Society of Australia
www.parrotsociety.org.au/articles/art_023.htm

Talk Parrots
www.talkparrots.com

World Parrot Trust
www.parrots.org/index.php/encyclopedia/profile/rainbow_
Lorikeet

Appendix 1 - CITES and Parrots

In 1973 the Convention on International Trade in Endangered Species of Wild Fauna and Flora was established to combat over-exploitation. Sadly, many baby parrots are stolen from their nests, sold and smuggled into the Unites States and other countries where they can command higher prices.

When you begin to look for your own bird, it's important to work with reputable breeders who maintain active aviaries. Be cautious of anyone who has a single bird for sale. Try to find out the parrot's origin before making a purchase. Your desire is to support the species, not the illegal trade in exotic animals. Please exercise extreme caution when buying your companion bird online. This can expose them to dangerous conditions when being shipped and you must ensure that this has been addressed by the breeder and carrier.

If you are interested in actively supporting the conservation of parrot species in the wild, see the World Parrot Trust's website at www.parrots.org.

The following list are birds covered under CITES that are facing the danger of extinction. They can only be traded under very specific certification, and for the hobbyist, the vast majority of offers to purchase any of these species should be regarded as potentially illegal.

For further information regarding CITES and parrots, in the UK contact: Department for Environment, Food and Rural Affairs - 0117 372 8749. Open 9 a.m. to 5 p.m. www.defra.gov.uk

Or in the United States of America: U.S. Fish and Wildlife Service, 1-800-344-WILD. Open 8:00 a.m. to 8:00 p.m. Eastern Time, Monday through Friday. www.fws.gov

Endangered Parrot Species are listed as:

Amazona arausiaca – Red-necked Amazon
Amazona barbadensis – Yellow-shouldered Amazon
Amazona brasiliensis – Red-tailed Amazon
Amazona finschi – Lilac-crowned Amazon
Amazona guildingii – St Vincent Amazon
Amazona imperialis – Imperial Amazon
Amazona leucocephala – Cuban Amazon
Amazona ochrocephala auropalliata – Yellow-crowned Amazon
Amazona ochrocephala belizensis – Double Yellow-headed Amazon (Belize)
Amazona ochrocephala caribaea – Double Yellow-headed Amazon (Caribaea)
Amazona ochrocephala oratrix – Double Yellow-headed Amazon
Amazona ochrocephala parvipes – Yellow-naped Amazon
Amazona ochrocephala tresmariae – Double Yellow-headed Amazon (Tres Marias)

Amazona pretrei – Red-spectacled Amazon
Amazona rhodocorytha – Rhodocorytha Amazon
Amazona tucumana – Tucuman Amazon
Amazona versicolor – Saint Lucia Amazon
Amazona vinacea – Vinaceous Amazon
Amazona viridigenalis – Green-cheeked Amazon
Amazona vittata – Puerto Rican Amazon
Anodorhynchus hyacinthinus – Hyacinth macaw
Anodorhynchus leari – Lears macaw
Ara ambigua – Great-green macaw (Buffons)
Ara glaucogularis – Blue-throated macaw
Ara macao – Scarlet macaw
Ara maracana – Illiger's macaw
Ara militaris – Military macaw
Ara rubrogenys – Red-fronted macaw
Cacatua goffini – Goffins Cockatoo
Cacatua haematuropygia – Red-vented Cockatoo
Cacatua moluccensis – Moluccan Cockatoo
Cacatua sulphurea – Lesser Sulphur-crested/Yellow crested Cockatoo
Cacatua sulphurea abbitti – Abbots Lesser Sulphur-crested Cockatoo
Cacatua sulphurea parvula – Lesser Sulphur-crested Timor Cockatoo
Cacatua sulphurea citrinocristata – Citron-crested Cockatoo
Cyanopsitta spixii – Spix's macaw
Cyanoramphus forbesi – Chatham Island yellow-fronted parakeet
Cyanoramphus novaezelandiae – Red-fronted parakeet

Cyclopsitta diophthalma – Coxen Coxen's double-eyed fig parrot

Eos histrio – Red and blue lory

Eunymphicus cornutus – Horned parakeet

Geopsittacus occidentalis – Night parrot

Guarouba guarouba – Golden Conure

Neophema chrysogaster – Orange-bellied parrot

Ognorhynchus icterotis – Yellow-eared parrot

Pezoporus wallicus – Ground parrot

Pionopsitta pileata – Pileated parrot

Probosciger aterrimus – Palm Cockatoo

Propyrruha Couloni (formerly Ara Couloni) – Blue-headed macaw

Propyrruha Maracana (formerly Ara Maracana) – Blue-winged macaw

Psephotus chrysopterygius – Golden-shouldered parrot

Psephotus dissimilis – Hooded parrot

Psephotus pulcherrimus – Paradise parrot

Psittacula echo – Mauritus parakeet

Psittacula krameri (Ghana) – Ring-necked parakeet

Pyrrhura cruentata – Blue-throated parakeet

Rhynchopsitta pachyrhyncha – Thick-billed parrot

Rhynchopsitta terrisi – Maroon-fronted parakeet

Strigops habroptilus – Kakapo

Vini ultramarina – Ultramarine Lorikeet

You can get more information at this website www.cites.org

Selected Works Cited

Avian Medicine List: Basic Information Sheet for Lory and Lorikeet
www.lafebervet.com/avian-medicine-list/basic-information-sheets-for-the-lory-and-Lorikeet/

The Basics of Living with a Parrot
http://jamiesparrothelp.wordpress.com/2011/12/16/the-basics-of-living-with-a-parrot/

Iron Storage Disease / Hemochromatosis. Avian Web.
www.avianweb.com/ironstoragedisease.html

"Lories and Lorikeets." Love Your Parrot.
www.loveyourparrot.com/loryandLorikeet.html

Lorikeets. Burke's Backyard.
www.burkesbackyard.com.au/2001/archives/2001_archives/roadtests/birds?p=1200

Lorikeet Disease and Health Program. Avian Web.
www.avianweb.com/Lorikeethealthprogram.html

Lory and Lorikeet Care Sheet.
www.petco.com/assets/caresheets/bird/lory-and-Lorikeet.pdf

Moustaki, Nikki. *Parrots for Dummies*. For Dummies, 2005.
O'Connor, Rebecca K. "10 Facts About Living with Parrots."
www.birdchannel.com/bird-species/find-the-right-bird/facts-about-parrots.aspx

O'Connor, Rebecca K. *Lories and Lorikeets: The Birdkeepers' Guide*. TFH Publications, 2011.

Rainbow Lorikeet. Australian Wildlife. www.australianwildlife.com.au/rainbow.htm

Rainbow Lorikeet. World Parrot Trust. www.parrots.org/index.php/encyclopedia/profile/rainbow_Lorik eet/

Schroeder, Dick. "Your 15 Lory Questions Answered: Discover What Sets Lories Apart from Other Parrots." Bird Channel. October 2008. www.birdchannel.com/bird-magazines/bird-talk/2008-october/fifteen-lory-questions-answered.aspx

Schroeder, Dick. "Hormonal and Aggressive Lories and Lorikeets: Learn the Signs of a Hormonal and Aggressive Lory or Lorikeet and When to Expect Aggression." Bird Channel. www.birdchannel.com/bird-behavior-and-training/aggressive-lories-and-Lorikeets.aspx

Stevens, Paul. "Breeding and Caring for Lorikeets." Hunger Valley Avicultural Society. www.hvas.asn.au/Lorikeets.html

Glossary

Allergy – An allergy is a negative immune response in a sensitive individual triggered by a foreign substance like pet dander. Reactions to pet dander are specific by species, so a person who is allergic to cats would not necessarily be allergic to any other animal. Typical symptoms include itching, watering eyes, sneezing, and varying degrees of respiratory distress.

Avian specialist – A veterinarian who has been trained to specialize in the treatment of companion birds.

Aviary bird – Birds that live in large outdoor enclosures in captivity and that may or may not be handled on a routine basis by humans.

Beak – The upper and lower jaws or mandibles of birds come together to form their beaks. Also referred to as a "bill."

Beaking – This is an exploratory behavior seen in all species of parrots. The bird will use its bill to investigate something that has attracted its attention. Beaking is often mistaken as aggression or biting, but in reality is an expression of curiosity. Rainbow Lorikeets will also taste whatever they find intriguing.

Bird fancier's lung – This is the common name for the allergic disease hypersensitivity pneumonitis, which can develop after long-term exposure to bird dander. The condition presents with few symptoms beyond a dry cough until it enters the chronic stage when fever, chills, and seriously diminished respiratory capacity strike. Permanent lung damage will result if the condition is not treated.

Breast - The region of a bird's body lying just below the throat.

Cere – The fleshy patch above a bird's beak where the nostrils are located.

Crop – This organ, which can be compared to a sack, lies between a bird's esophagus and stomach. Food goes through a preliminary stage of digestion there before moving lower in the digestive tract.

Crown - This term refers to the topmost portion of a bird's head.

Ears – Located just behind the eyes, a bird's ears are two small openings on the side of the head that, in healthy animals, are always hidden beneath a fine layer of feathers.

Eyes – Bird's eyes are located on either side of their heads for the evolutionary purpose of providing the creature with a maximum field of vision to aid in locating food and avoiding predators.

Fear aggression – Any aggressive behavior including biting, which is a response to an event, including a sound or motion, which has frightened any animal, including birds.

HEPA filter - HEPA is the acronym for "High Efficiency Particulate Air" filter. When used with a vacuum cleaner, a HEPA filter can remove 99.97% of all particles in the air as small as just tens of a micrometer. HEPA filters are extremely useful in controlling levels of pet dander present in a household.

Hormonal aggression – Hormonal aggression is seen in many species of companion birds as they are reaching sexual maturity and is roughly analgous to the emotional upset of adolescence in humans.

Learned aggression – Aggressive behaviors that a bird engages in for the express purpose of eliciting a desired response are said to be learned aggression. Basically, the bird comes to understand that by displaying ill temper, he will get what he wants.

Lorikeet (Lory) - These two terms are used interchangeably for a widely varied collection of brightly colored, medium sized parrots indigenous to the islands of the South Pacific, Asia, and Australia. The Rainbow Lorikeet is one of the most popular of these birds kept as a companion animal.

Mantle - The descriptive term for a bird's back.

Nape - The descriptive term for the back of a bird's neck.

Nictating membrane - A thin, semi-transparent "third" eyelid that passes over the surface of a bird's eye to protect, lubricate, and clean the surface of the eye.

Parrot – Parrots are tropical birds in the family Psittacidae. Typically they are brightly colored and have short, hooked beaks. Many species of parrots have the ability to mimic human speech.

Parrot fever – A bird disease caused by the bacterium Chlamydia psittici, which can be passed to humans. If untreated in humans, 15 to 20% of cases prove fatal.

Pet bird – Any bird living with and interacting with humans on a daily basis. Commonly referred to as "companion birds."

Primary feathers – The wing feathers of a bird that allow for flight. There are ten primary feathers in total.

Rump – This is the area beneath the bird's primary flight feathers located on the lower back.

Secondary feathers - The feathers of the wing located closer to the body and lying under the primary feathers.

Territorial aggression – Aggressive behavior exhibited by animals, including birds, triggered by someone or something invading what the creature perceives to be its territory.

Training aids – Any device used to help a human teach or train an animal, including a bird, to exhibit a desired behavior or to give a desired response.

Vent - The area under a bird's tail feathers for elimination. Birds defecate, but they do not urinate.

Zoonotic – A disease that can be transmitted from an animal to a human being

Index

A

adoption 20, 23, 33
aggressive 10, 22, 40, 43, 63, 67, 70, 127, 142, 143
allergic alveolitis 91
aspergillosis 82, 83
avian influenza 92
avian vet/avian vets/avian veterinarian/avian veterinarians 7,
33, 76, 93, 94, 95, 96, 103, 108, 114, 118, 119
aviary 5, 23, 32, 33, 40, 49, 50, 57, 66, 67, 87, 102, 124, 140
aviculture 5, 10, 132
aviculturists 2, 9, 13, 24, 36, 37

B

bacterial and yeast infections 47, 88
baking soda 60, 101
bath/bathing 56, 60, 65, 72, 104, 127
beak/beaks 5,
6, 11, 15, 52, 53, 54, 70, 71, 72, 73, 76, 78, 86, 103, 105, 113, 130, 140, 141, 143
bird flu 92
blooming eucalyptus flowers 14
BPA/BPA free 47, 51
breeding 16, 39, 106, 107, 108, 109, 114
brooder 109, 110, 111, 128

C

cage/cages..5, 6, 13, 21, 35, 37, 38, 39, 41, 44, 45, 46, 47, 48, 49, 50, 51, 55, 56, 57, 58, 59, 60, 61, 65, 66, 71, 72, 78, 79, 82, 85, 90, 100, 101, 102, 103, 114, 120, 123, 124, 125, 128, 129, 130
cage cleaning 59, 101
cage maintenance...101
candidiasis 88, 89
cere..76, 141
chicks............................5, 18, 107, 108, 109, 110, 111, 112, 114, 115
chlamydiosis...84, 86
CITES.. 134,135
companion bird/companion birds 5, 6, 20, 36, 38, 45, 49, 50, 59, 66, 76, 90, 92, 93, 99, 108, 114, 125, 127, 128, 140, 142
conure...5
crop/crops 5, 14, 89, 110, 111, 112, 141
cuttlebone 6, 53, 54, 103

D

dander pneumoconiosis...91
diet/diets 2, 10, 11, 20, 21, 33, 41, 51, 52, 53, 55, 75, 80, 81, 100, 101, 102, 103, 112, 119, 124, 130
discharge... 32, 76, 77, 80, 83, 85, 105
disinfectants...60
DNA 16, 106, 114
doxycycline...85
drinking water 55, 72, 79, 88

E

eggs.. 107, 109, 115

F

feather plucking 66, 86, 87, 121

feathers... 6,
32, 36, 58, 67, 68, 70, 72, 73, 77, 78, 79, 83, 85, 86, 87, 105, 107, 111, 141, 143, 144

feces 2, 3, 13, 39, 44, 52, 59, 64, 65, 78, 83, 90, 124, 129

feet 11, 51, 72, 78, 86, 105, 130

female/females 15, 106, 107

flock/flocks...1, 12, 13, 40, 59, 81, 107, 123, 127

flowers... 10, 14, 128

free flying..6, 128

free flying time 65

G

grooming 73, 87, 127

H

H5N1 ....92, 93

haemochromatosis..81

hand-raised... 5, 18, 43, 107

hanging toys..102

health.....................7, 20, 33, 51, 53, 72, 73, 75, 80, 81, 86, 92, 93, 96, 97, 98, 120, 124

health problems 80, 98, 120

HEPA filter 90, 142

herpes viruses 84

hormonal aggression.. 6, 23, 60, 142

household chemicals 60

husbandry..5

I

illegal trade..134
inTune 112
iron.. 21, 53, 80, 81, 87, 103
iron overload 80, 81
iron storage disease 53, 80, 87, 103

J

jaw/jaws 5, 11, 53, 140
juvenile rainbow lorikeets 15

K

Kaytee..112

L

ladders.. 50, 66, 102
lamp...58, 110
lava stone 54, 103
LeFeber...112
leg disease..86
leg/legs 11, 71, 72, 78, 86, 105, 114, 130
lethargic 79, 83
lifespan...43, 118
liver disease...87
loriinae 8
lory.. 2, 6, 9, 14, 126, 142

M

males..15, 70, 106

mates 67

medical care...80

mineral block/mineral blocks...54, 103

mites 86, 87, 89

N

nails 11

nap/naps 66, 72, 78, 105

nares 76

nectar...........................2, 9, 10, 11, 13, 21, 33, 51, 52, 75, 80, 100, 101, 113, 124, 130

nectar mix/nectar mixes...52, 53, 102

nesting..72, 107, 130

nostrils..76, 83, 141

nutrition 9, 21, 75, 80, 81

nutritional deficiencies...87

O

open beak...73

Oral Rehydration Solution (UK)...111

outdoor aviary/outdoor aviaries...40, 49, 66, 124

P

pacheco's disease...83, 84

papillae..10, 11

parasites...86, 88

parrot/parrots........ ....1, 2, 3, 6, 8, 9, 11, 13, 14, 20, 21, 36, 42,
    43, 46, 47, 62, 81, 83, 84, 106, 118, 119, 120, 121, 124, 127, 131, 134, 140, 142, 143

Pedialyte (US)..111

pellet/pellets 9, 21, 51, 81, 102

perch/perches 37, 38, 47, 48, 50, 51, 59, 64, 65, 66, 68, 72, 76, 79, 102, 105, 130

pet insurance 96, 97, 98

plumage 6, 78

pollen.. 9, 10, 11

potty training 63

preening... 72, 73

psittacidae.. 8, 143

S

scaly face... 86

screams... 23

screeches 23

seed/seeds 5, 9, 11, 21, 48, 51, 75, 80, 81, 102, 113, 130

sexual maturity 106, 142

shopping 46, 97, 131

skin irritation.. 87, 90

socialization.. 6, 59, 60, 71, 103

squawking 73

sub-species.. 9, 10

swings 50, 102

T

temperature range 58

The Association of Avian Veterinarians (US) at AAV.org 94

The International Union for Conservation of Nature (IUCN) 14

tongue/tongues 10, 11, 70, 71, 113

travel carrier 57

V

vegetables 21, 52, 53, 55, 75, 80, 81, 101, 102, 130
ventilation...87
vet/vets/veterinarian/veterinarians..............................7, 20, 33, 53, 57, 68, 76, 78, 79, 80, 82, 83, 87, 89, 93, 94, 95, 96, 97, 98, 102, 103, 108, 114, 118, 119, 140
vinegar 60, 101
vitamin supplementation 53, 103
vocal 22, 23, 35, 36

W

water............................2, 11, 41, 55, 56, 57, 59, 72, 79, 83, 88, 101, 104, 127
wing clipping 36, 37, 38
wing/wings.............................6, 14, 36, 37, 38, 47, 58, 72, 73, 90, 105, 130, 143
World Parrot Trust..143

Z

zoonotic...7, 20, 84, 92, 144
ZuPreem 112

Photo Credits

Cover Design:- Liliana Gonzalez Garcia, ipublicidades.com (info@ipublicidades.com)

Page 4 By Brisbane City Council www.flickr.com/photos/brisbanecitycouncil/8065738622/sizes/l

Page 10 By Mats Lindh (originally posted to Flickr as IMG_5046) via Wikimedia Commons http://commons.wikimedia.org/wiki/File%3ARainbow_Lorikeet_(Trichoglossus_haematodus)_-drinking.jpg

Page 15 By John Dalton (Own work) via Wikimedia Commons http://commons.wikimedia.org/wiki/File%3ARainbow_Lorikeet_Pair_on_Brampton_Island.jpg

Page 22 By darrell.barrell (en:Image:Rainbow-lorikeet-closeup-eating-apple.jpg) [Public domain], via Wikimedia Commons http://commons.wikimedia.org/wiki/File%3ARainbow-lorikeet-closeup-eating-apple.jpg

Page 37 By Louise Docker from Sydney, Australia (Lorikeet in flight) via Wikimedia Commons
http://commons.wikimedia.org/wiki/File%3ARainbow_Lorikeet_in_flight.jpg

Page 56 By dicktay2000
www.flickr.com/photos/34094515@N00/3817086937/sizes/o/

Page 65 By PsJeremy
www.flickr.com/photos/psjeremy/8303594868/sizes/l/

Page 69 By rexboggs5
www.flickr.com/photos/rexboggs5/1490382326/

Page 77 By Andrew Morrell Photography
www.flickr.com/photos/andrewmorrell/108956116/sizes/o/

Page 99 By aussiegall
www.flickr.com/photos/aussiegall/1340184477/sizes/o/

Page 104 By Nitevision
www.flickr.com/photos/octavaria/278071767/sizes/l/

Page 106 By aussiegall
www.flickr.com/photos/aussiegall/1264945559/sizes/o/

Page 115 By Takver
www.flickr.com/photos/takver/9212235617/sizes/l/

Page 123 By Alex Proimos
www.fotopedia.com/items/flickr-6760627561

Page 126 By Richard Fisher
www.flickr.com/photos/richardfisher/3012436508/sizes/l/

Page 131 Image courtesy www.tropicalbirdshop.com

All Creative Commons work

These works are licensed under the Creative Commons Attribution 2.0 Generic license and 3.0 Unported License. To view a copy of this license, visit http://creativecommons.org/licenses/by/3.0/ or send a letter to Creative Commons, 444 Castro Street, Suite 900, Mountain View, California, 94041, USA. (cc) BY

All other photos – www.bigstockphotos.com

Inside cover, Pages 1, 8, 12, 17, 19, 34, 45, 52, 55, 61, 67, 73, 75, 82, 89, 117.

CPSIA information can be obtained at www.ICGtesting.com
Printed in the USA
LVOW01s2120030414

380282LV00008B/21/P